Three-Shot Golf For Women

Three-Shot Golf
For Women

by

JANET COLES, LPGA

SANDRA FOSTER, PH.D.

PHOTOGRAPHS BY JAMES TOLLEY

BURFORD BOOKS

To Fred Wetmore, who taught me how to play golf.

To my parents, for supporting me the way they did.

Printed in the United States of America

10 9 8 7 6 5 4 3 2 1

Library of Congress Cataloging-in-Publication Data

Coles, Janet, 1954–
    Three-shot golf for women / by Janet Coles, Sandra Foster.
       p. cm.
    Includes biblioghraphical references (p.) and index.
    ISBN 1-58080-032-7 (pb)
    1. Golf for women. 2. Golf—Study and teaching. I. Foster, Sandra, 1950–   , II. Title.
    GV966.C65   1999
    796.352'082—dc21   98-52417
                                                   CIP

Contents

Playing Great Golf in Record Time

I'm a former LPGA touring professional with a fine career record behind me. Now, like some others who have retired from the tour, I'm the author of an instructional book. What makes me a different author, and this a different book, is that I can teach you to play respectable bogey golf if you're a beginner, or great golf if you're a more advanced player in less time than you ever thought possible.

Let me explain how.

My passion for golf came from my love of sports, my desire to better myself as an athlete, and the good fortune to have grown up next to a golf course. I started playing at the age of nine, competed almost immediately, then became a junior champion, a ranked amateur, and a collegiate player. Just one month after I graduated from the University of California at Los Angeles (UCLA), I qualified for the LPGA tour. As a determined rookie, I rapidly developed into a contender and went on to win my first LPGA tournament within a year.

My passions for competition and the game were so strong that I worked incredibly hard, took risks, and stayed focused. I wanted to better myself every day so that I could compete successfully. This combination resulted in tournament wins and impressive earnings over a career that spanned twelve years.

Now my passion for golf is different. I have made the transition from player to teacher. These are two very separate roles, and I have totally embraced the *latter*. At this point in my career, my greatest pleasure comes from teaching golfers at all levels how to play the game better.

More recently, I have recognized the need for a curriculum that focuses exclusively on the needs of women when they play the game of golf. Because women often have multiple responsibilities, they must allocate their time carefully. I take this fact seriously, and have designed time-saving strategies tailored just for them. Many women, in meeting the demands of raising children and/or developing their careers, find their golf-playing days interrupted, perhaps for many months, even years. These women need a system that rewards them for whatever hours they can devote to the game. Three-Shot Golf is a system that emphasizes certain shots to help beginners become successful quickly, and allow returnees and seasoned players to rapidly improve their scores.

I have come up with drills and homework practice assignments that women can complete without having to go to the driving range. These away-from-the-golf-course drills can enhance a woman's skill without her having to hit golf balls for hours and hours. Underlying all that I recommend is my respect for the many roles that women have in caring for their partners or spouses, their children, and their parents—a situation unique to women. My advice and strategies are therefore designed to accommodate the busy lifestyle of so many women, so they can stay in the game.

I'm not saying that men aren't busy. I've played golf with extremely busy corporate executives and professionals. I know about the demands of work on men.

What is unique to women, however, is the pressure of *multiple* roles and the responsibility for the direct or day-to-day care of others, usually without anyone to regularly delegate that responsibility to. When a woman's time is divided in so many ways, she can easily find herself thinking she might have to give up her golfing, or not even start lessons. That's why I have concentrated my efforts as an instructor on determining the ways that beginners can be successful quickly, and that women returning to the game when their children are older can get reinvolved rapidly and happily. And even when children are grown, and women can devote more leisure time to the game, they want strategies that lower their scores and offer them a respectable-looking game.

Three-Shot Golf meets all of these needs by teaching you, in an efficient manner, the best shots for amateur women players. In this book I bring to you, the female reader and player, my enthusiasm as a teacher and my dedication to helping you meet the challenges of learning this demanding sport—with a conceptual approach that can get you going and keep you in the game.

I have started hundreds of beginners and coached many tournament winners from New York to San Francisco. Having taught so many newcomers to golf, I've concluded that the instructional emphasis should be different for women than it is for men. Men's books and lessons emphasize putting and technical swing mechanics, with a goal of "hitting it far." Men and their instructors emphasize getting more yards on a full swing.

That makes sense for men but not for women. Most male players can learn to hit the ball far enough to make par. It's true that when they first achieve the needed yardage, they may not be making par; still, they're hitting the ball far enough to get it onto the green in the regulation number of strokes. Therefore, I work with male students on their accuracy.

Women won't succeed at golf if they focus on swing mechanics and distance the way men do. They're simply much less likely to gain distance than men are. They need other strategies.

I tackle the issue of distance in a way that's different from most instructors, both male and female. Many instructors encourage female players to "just hit it far." For the majority of the women I've worked with, though, the distance from tee to pin is intimidating. I don't find that telling women to "hit it far" is the most effective teaching strategy. Instead, I suggest learning to hit the ball off the tee far *enough*—155 yards, an attainable goal, and far enough to play bogey golf.

The seasoned players who have come to me for help were women who could already hit the ball this far but were still shooting 110. The advice "just hit it farther" hadn't helped them improve. Even when they'd added yards to their tee shot, their scores didn't necessarily go down. I've seen women who could hit the ball 180 yards off the tee and still struggled with high scores—before they started lessons with me. What I gave them was a system that focused their efforts differently, at specific shots, hit solidly, in a consistent manner. That helped them lower their scores and took their minds off the preoccupation with distance.

I've had the privilege of playing with many women at numerous golf courses across the United States. I've found repeatedly that it isn't just a distance issue that keeps women from lowering their scores. When I noted that the women who tried to hit the ball harder to make it go farther weren't getting the results they wanted, it became clear to me that they needed to hit the ball solidly, more of the time. So I incorporated into my system tactics for becoming more consistent with a full swing, in order to advance the ball.

When women learn to hit the ball solidly, they are developing a better full swing. So I concentrate on consistent, solid ball contact. In my experience, this yields better results than trying to get more speed and distance. When women hit a solid golf shot, they can feel it. "That's golf," I say, and they agree. In contrast, focusing on distance can become the number one swing wrecker.

Most women think that when they break 100, they're golfers. I agree. However, by definition, a person shooting in the 90s is still learning more about how to swing and how to play the game. When I begin with a student, I tell her that there are four aspects to playing golf:

1. Twenty-five percent of golf is mastering the full swing, including fairway wood shots and shots with the driver and irons.

2. Twenty-five percent is the short game—getting into the "scoring zone"—with miniature swings like the pitch, sand shots, and strokes like putting and chipping.

3. Twenty-five percent is the mental attitude or mental strategies helpful in playing golf.

4. Twenty-five percent is using the right equipment for you.

If you concentrate most of your time on just the full swing, you're overlooking 75 percent of the game. So I encourage women to look beyond lessons on full swing.

So what's my plan for you women players beyond these lessons on full swing?

My Three-Shot Golf system teaches you three primary shots to make your game successful: a 30-yard **pitch shot**[1] that gets onto the green every time; an impressive **tee shot** that goes the distance I just mentioned; and a respectable **fairway wood shot,** generally using a 5-wood. These are the three shots you'll need for most holes. These three shots are my winning formula that'll get beginners to play bogey golf quickly. For those of you who have broken

---

[1] I have prepared a glossary of golf terms for you that also includes a selection of sports psychology terms. When you see a boldfaced word in the text, you'll find it defined in the glossary.

90, these are still your three most important shots. Even when you break 85, these three shots will serve you well.

How is this system different from what's usually taught to men—and to most women? Men have less need for the pitch shot. They do better to concentrate on gaining distance, which is more within their reach, and improving their sand play and long-distance putting.

Women are well aware that they won't get to par golf easily, because of the distances involved, but they may still have been taught to try to get onto the greens like men can. What I suggest as a great alternative is this: Take an advancement shot, a 110-yard shot down the fairway with a 5- or 7-wood, and then pitch onto the green. You can play bogey golf by using a 30- to 50-yard pitch shot on almost every hole.

I believe that I have made significant improvement in the way women are taught, both as beginners and as seasoned players desiring improvement, with my emphasis on approaching the greens through pitching. Unfortunately, many golf courses, learning centers, and driving ranges don't have an area where you can work on pitch shots. However, I maintain that this is a crucial shot for women, and one worth finding an appropriate place to practice.

> THREE-SHOT GOLF IS A CONCEPTUAL SYSTEM FOR LEARNING GOLF QUICKLY AS A BEGINNER. IT IS A SYSTEM FOR ADVANCED GOLFERS TO LOWER SCORES BY FOCUSING ON SHOTS THAT ARE STROKE SAVERS.

My students learn a way to practice that saves them valuable time. This book teaches you how to do these drills. Each practice session is targeted specifically and concisely to save you precious hours. Also, my students learn how *not* to practice failure. Likewise, you will discover how to avoid repeating things that don't work—like practicing shots that you rarely use, or spending your effort and time on techniques that don't give the female player good results.

I know that you have a career, a family, and other interests, and you could probably use some hours all to yourself, too. So I have devised a way for you to save time and still improve. In Three-Shot Golf I teach you to efficiently practice the three shots of most importance to you. I explain how to schedule your practice sessions, using your driving-range time in the most efficient manner.

I teach you *attainable* distance goals—not trying to hit it "farther."

You, the beginner, can learn a respectable tee shot. I'll show you how to hit one, and how far. If you already have a good tee shot, I have tips that will allow you to hit it consistently so that it's *really* impressive.

Even though it's overlooked or underrated in other instructional books, the pitch shot can become your secret weapon, like it is for my students. Getting your 30-, 40-, or 50-yard approach shot onto the green every time is a primary goal in Three-Shot Golf. It's not that I think putting is unimportant. But it's obvious that your putting skill will be all the more valuable when you can get to the green quickly and reliably.

These shots are terrific for those of you who have been playing for a long time but feel that your game is "stuck." Three-Shot Golf can help you move off that plateau and significantly reduce your score.

Also, for you experienced players, I remind you that golf is a game in which even the masters get challenged. Golf is complex enough that seasoned players can get it and lose it and get it back again. Many novice golfers start out by hitting the ball well but don't know how they're making it happen. Then they lose it and don't know what to do to get it back. You've probably had the experience of thinking, "I've got it!"—only to later lose it.

"It" comes and goes. As you become an avid golfer, the course will be both a place of frustration and one of elation when you figure out your swing problems.

I'll help you manage these difficulties; to see them as setbacks rather than as failures or a reason to sell your clubs. You'll learn how to pull out of the overthinking trap. This is what happens when players concentrate so hard on their golf mechanics that they get paralyzed by mistake analysis. The tips I'll give you don't have to be analyzed.

> IT'S FAIR TO SAY THAT NO ONE EVER ACHIEVES PERFECTION IN GOLF—NOT EVEN THE MASTERS. IN THIS BOOK YOU WON'T BE GOING AFTER PERFECT. YOU'LL BE LEARNING SKILLS THAT GET YOU TO BOGEY GOLF QUICKLY AS A BEGINNER, AND LOWER YOUR SCORES FAST AS A MORE ADVANCED PLAYER.

The heart of this book and of my Three-Shot Golf system is learning to get your 30-yard pitch shot onto the green *every* time. I guarantee lower scores as you improve this shot, which doesn't require youth, strength, or **clubhead speed** to master. It's a high-trajectory shot taken with a sand wedge, a pitching wedge, or another **lofted club** such as the **lob wedge,** the chic new club most women like to have in their bag. The pitch is a **miniature swing,** not a full swing. You beginners and novices can build your full swing from it.

When I teach Three-Shot Golf, I simplify the hundreds of instructions that most of my students were taught before they started taking lessons from me. I streamline what to do and how to think effectively about what you're doing. My instructions are straightforward and to the point. Your head won't be full of **angles of approach,** degrees of **loft,** or "Do this with your right elbow and left kneecap" as you swing.

When I observe a new student's play before she begins lessons with me, I frequently see that she is looking around, worried about what others on the course think of her playing. Instead of being mentally engaged, she is what I call physically distracted.

Because I know how crucial a woman's mental game is to her playing, I asked my friend and colleague Dr. Sandra Foster to help me with this book. "Sam" is a performance-enhancement psychologist who really understands how performance anxiety affects women both at work and when they take on a challenging athletic activity. Sam brings the latest sports-psychology techniques to you in sidebars scattered throughout my instructional chapters as well as in chapter 7, on mental attitude. These techniques will help you manage your thoughts and emotions so you can be mentally engaged whenever you pick up a club.

Golf is a great social game that can put you on the course for hours with the men and women who are your business associates, customers, and friends. Playing a decent game of golf has become a valuable business tool and social skill, and there's no reason you shouldn't make good use of it.

Likewise, you can use the time with your foursome for sharing stories, having fun, and building relationships. As a golfer, you can play against yourself and focus on the process of mastering new skills. Or golf can be your way to learn about healthy competition—often a foreign concept for women who attended high school and college before **Title IX** and consequently didn't have the opportunities for team-sport involvement and athletic scholarships that are available to young women today.

More women than ever are taking up golf—women like you. Unfortunately, many women quit before they attain the level of mastery they had hoped to reach. I want to change that with this book. If you're a beginner, I want you to learn to play well quickly and have some serious fun on the course, feeling at home there. If you're an experienced but frustrated player, Sam and I have important advice for staying mentally on track while reducing your score. I encourage you to go after bogey golf and then think about lowering your score even farther from there.

Here's an important thing to remember. Most of us tend to think that "par" is average and bogey is something below average. Get this concept out of your mind! In the *real* golf world, only expert players shoot par—probably less than 1 percent of all players, men and women. Women players in particular need to keep the positive mental attitude that bogey golf is not only attainable but also worthwhile. Bogey golf means shooting 90 on a par-72 course. Most players—men and women—almost never shoot this well.

To further illustrate just what I'm talking about with Three-Shot Golf, let's take an imaginary stroll onto the golf course with two friends, whom we'll call Sherry and Sarah.

Sherry has been playing golf for a couple of years and has better-than-average skills. She's a business-owner and mother of two and hasn't got much time to hone her golf game. Although she enjoys the rounds she gets in with her friend Sarah, and doesn't pay much attention to the score at the end of the round, she's frustrated by golf and has thought about letting it go. She thinks her skills should be getting her a better score and can't ever seem to get her entire game in sync. She usually shoots 110 for eighteen holes.

Sarah's game used to be a lot like Sherry's—an everyday game with some flaws in her approach that prevented her from playing her best golf. But she read this book, she worked on the Three-Shot Golf concept, and her game has improved.

Here's how they play:

The hole is a 405-yard par 4 that doglegs slightly to the left. There's a fairway bunker about 220 yards out to the right and a pair of bunkers astride the green, but otherwise there are no hazards.

Sherry takes out her driver and hits the ball 150 yards. It would have gone farther if it had been straight, but she slices the ball and it lands in rough to the right of the fairway.

Sarah also hits a driver. She isn't a long hitter but she concentrates on making a smooth, even swing. Her ball goes 140 yards, but stays in the middle of the fairway.

Sherry has tensed up as she approaches her second shot. She knows she needs a good shot here to recover, and pulls out her 3-wood, hoping to move the ball forward a good 160 yards, just short of the green. She's hit such a shot before . . . .

But not this time. Her 3-wood is hit fat, and the ball ends up on the left side of the fairway, about 90 yards in all.

Sarah moves up to her ball, takes out her favorite 7-wood, and gives it her smoothest swing. It isn't a spectacular shot—but she knows it doesn't have to be. The ball advances 125 yards, still in the center of the fairway.

Sherry is now in the fairway, at least, and with 160 yards or so to go to the green she thinks she has a shot at getting on if she can get her long irons to cooperate. She pulls out a 3-iron, willing to leave it short if she has to, and fires away. It's a good shot—at first. But then it tails off to the right and ends up just inside the right-hand bunker.

Sarah's next shot is almost a copy of her last—a smooth 7-wood, moving 125 yards down the fairway.

You can see what's happening. Sarah is playing the shots she knows and has practiced, while Sherry is hoping to hit the shot of her life with every swing. Sarah is up to her favorite distance now, about 50 yards from the pin, and she's practiced this shot so many times that her confidence is high as she lays the ball on the green and leaves it some 6 feet from the pin. She gets a little lucky on her putt, and makes it for a bogey 5. A good hole.

Sherry's greenside experience is much different. She manages to get out of the bunker, but just barely, leaving the ball in some fringe rough short of the putting surface. She chips, but the ball rolls to the opposite side of the green, a good 20 feet from the hole. She 2-putts from there—good putting in light of her high frustration level. She cards a 7.

Sherry has tried all the hard shots—shots even the pros have trouble with. She went for the big drive, needed a touch 3-wood from the rough, then a pinpoint 3-iron, a sand shot, a tough downhill chip, and a long putt. No wonder her score ballooned!

Sarah owes her bogey to the three shots she's practiced—her drive, her 7-wood, and her 50-yard pitch. That's Three-Shot Golf.

I strongly recommend that serious beginners commit themselves to a season of twelve weeks to learn golf—the equivalent of one summer. I encourage those of you just starting out to sign up for a golf school right away, or to seek a teaching professional. You advanced players will probably benefit from lessons as well, especially lessons that focus on these three shots. Find a professional with credentials who will help make real the tips in this book.

A good instructor is someone who plays well, has been through the rigorous training program of the **PGA** or **LPGA,** and enjoys teaching. This is someone who checks your implementation of drills like the ones in this book, and who gives you encouragement and perspective when things get tough. A good instructor also stays up to date on the latest teaching ideas.

Ask around for recommendations of instructors who get results for *women players*. If you don't know how or where to find a good teaching professional, contact the PGA office in Palm Beach Gardens, Florida (407-624-8400), or the LPGA Headquarters in Daytona Beach, Florida (904-254-8800).

> COMMIT YOURSELF TO LEARNING GOLF OR SIGNIFICANTLY IMPROVING YOUR GAME BY GIVING IT TWELVE WEEKS OF YOUR FOCUSED ATTENTION.

I recommend that you practice hitting balls in front of your instructor in order to get the feedback you need to progress more quickly. In my opinion, using your lesson time solely to watch your instructor show you new skills is not as effective as also devoting some of those minutes to practicing your shots.

In chapter 1, I'll go over the fundamentals of Three-Shot Golf. For you seasoned players, check the suggestions and techniques in this chapter to see if there are any adjustments that you want to make.

CHAPTER ONE

Fundamentals of Three-Shot Golf

1 EQUIPMENT

As you might guess, proper equipment is very important. As a beginner, however, you don't need fourteen clubs in your bag. Eventually—as you improve—you will require a full set.

When you buy clubs, pay attention to the flexibility of the **clubshaft** and to the length of the clubs. I teach many younger women who are 5 feet, 9 inches tall and who swing pretty hard. But right now there are no golf clubs made specifically for them. A student like this might find that the clubs designed for senior players work for her, but I steer her away from buying one that says SENIOR in big letters on the shaft. Another option for her and for you is purchasing custom-fitted golf clubs.

You can get your club specifications measured at an upscale store that sells clubs and other equipment and purchase your clubs there (and sometimes their prices *aren't* higher). Or you can see a club fitter, a professional whose only job is to fit and sell clubs, and buy from him or her. Another option is to go, with your specifications in hand, to a discount golf supplier and buy clubs off the shelf. I really think that you'll be glad that you own clubs matched to your swing and skill level.

There is so-called game-improvement golf equipment now available, and you can benefit from this new technology. Choose clubs with flexible clubshafts made of **graphite,** which moves the ball farther and makes your game more enjoyable. The graphite-shafted clubs are also lighter and easier to swing.

The **titanium** drivers and **fairway woods** give you a bigger **sweet spot,** and the heavier weight at the bottom of the **clubhead** makes the ball go into the air more quickly so that the **trajectory** is there. The bigger the sweet spot, the more likely you are to get **centeredness of hit** and, therefore, more distance. Anything that makes the sweet spot bigger is better.

Your first equipment purchases should consist of a **pitching wedge** and a fairway wood that you love, probably a 5-wood. You will also need a 5-iron through a **sand wedge.** Be sure you buy a short **putter;** otherwise, you won't lean over as far as the proper **setup** requires. As of this writing, no company makes putters designed exclusively for women.

I'm a believer in walking the golf course whenever possible, and I always use **caddies** when they are available. However, I think it's important for you to be able to carry your own bag. So choose one that's lightweight, in a neutral color. A great bag feature is a little stand that allows the bag to stay upright by itself.

1 BASICS

THE GRIP

Let's start with basics, beginning with the grip. I teach my students the one that I've found most effective for women: the overlapping grip. In the next few paragraphs I'll describe what right-handed players do in this grip; you lefties need to make adjustments accordingly.

First, place your left thumb against the knuckle of your left index finger as if they were zipped together, as in figure 1. If you can pinch a tee into the zipped space and hold it in place, you're doing this correctly. Now, coming from above, slip the club onto your left hand at the base of your fingers, with more of the club resting on your fingers than on your left palm. This allows your left wrist to hinge.

The **anatomical snuffbox** at the base of your thumb is recognizable as the little indentation between the two ligaments that's visible when you arch your thumb back toward your wrist. Align your left-hand snuffbox over the top of the club, using the grip logo as a reference point. You should be able to look down and see first three knuckles of your left hand. The placement of your left hand establishes a guide for the correct placement of your right hand, and controls the **clubface,** as in figure 2.

Secure your right hand on the backside of the club, sliding it down the shaft so that it fits into your left thumb. The palm of your right hand should be at the backside of the grip, so that the palm can push the club at impact (see figure 3). As a check, take your right-hand index finger and slip it down the back of the shaft. If that finger goes to the back of the grip without your palm moving, then you have your right hand in the proper place. If you've got your right hand too far under the grip, your right index finger, when extended, will be at the bottom of the grip, and you'll notice

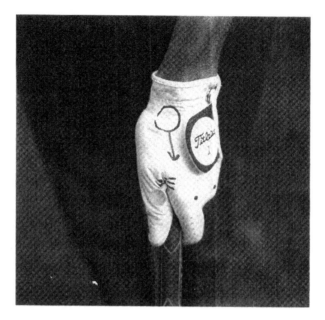

Fig. 1. *Proper left-hand grip. The left thumb "zips" flat against the base knuckle of the index finger. You should be able to hold a tee in the zipped space. The "snuff box," circled at the top, should align with the top of the shaft.*

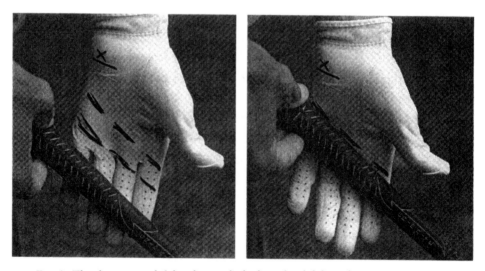

Fig. 2. *The glove on my left hand is marked where the club lies when your grip is correct. As your hand closes around the club, the heel of your palm, marked with an X, should be on top of the club.*

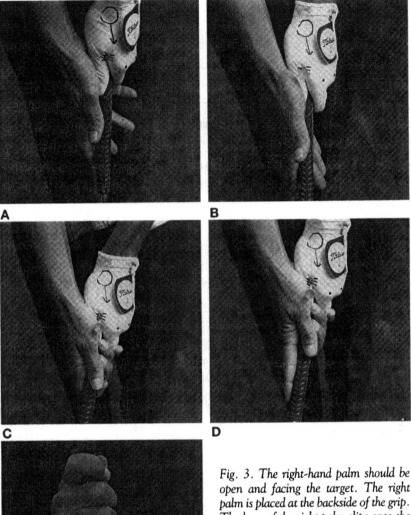

Fig. 3. The right-hand palm should be open and facing the target. The right palm is placed at the backside of the grip. The base of the right palm slips onto the left thumb. The "zipper" on the right hand remains zipped. As a checkpoint for the correct placement of the right hand, if you extend your right index finger down the back of the shaft, it should naturally extend to the backside of the grip. The right-hand pinkie should overlap the left forefinger knuckle. This creates the overlapping grip.

that it's in the wrong position. To correct this, move your right hand to the backside of the grip until it's in the right place.

Grip pressure should not be so tight that it prevents your wrist from hinging. The **wrist hinge** is one of the three **power generators** in golf and an important element in creating **leverage.** I tell my students what I learned from my master teacher, Jim Flick: Grip with secure fingers and relaxed arms. Grip pressure does vary in accordance with the weight of the club; the heavier the club, the firmer the grip. With a lighter club, the grip pressure is correspondingly lighter. Your putter is the heaviest club, so you use your firmest grip pressure on it. The driver is the lightest club, and you should use essentially a soft-hands grip.

Try this test: You should be able to lift the golf clubhead off the ground by putting a little hinge in your wrist and making little circles with the clubhead. You need the wrist action that comes from having a grip pressure that's not too tight.

Once I was teaching a woman student how to release the golf club. She was struggling with grip pressure, with holding her hands very tightly on the golf club. Her grip was so tight that the result was a lack of clubhead speed through to impact. I was trying to get her to soften up her forearms to lighten her grip pressure; I wanted her fingers secure on the club and her arms relaxed.

So I was teaching her how to get the club to swing a bit more in her hands, wrists, and arms so she wouldn't have to "push" the club. I said, "You've got to release your hands and release the golf club," while showing her kinesthetically what I meant. I realized that she was an auditory learner when on her next shot, she did release the golf club—which flew about 50 feet across the driving range!

I came away from that lesson with my lesson learned: A student may take what I say, in my amusing golf-jargon way, *quite* literally. It's taught me to be careful choosing what words I use to explain a skill.

THE SETUP

The next fundamental is **posture.** In my experience a correct posture writes the formula for a good **backswing,** and your backswing (or **takeaway**) writes the formula for your entire swing. There are two components of posture: a big bend and a slight flex, *in that order.*

The bend is from the hips; imagine that you are bowing, but from the hips, not the waist. To help them bend properly, I remind my students that the waist is not a joint. To achieve the proper bend, stand up straight with the palms of both hands on the tops

Fig. 4. Proper posture is the foundation of a good swing. To get a feel for the correct posture, stand straight, then bend at the hips, with your hands pressing the tops of your thighs back.

of your thighs. Push your thighs back to get into the appropriate hip bend (as shown in figure 4).

Your eyes, shoulders, hips, thighs, and knees all face the **target line.** The width of your **stance** will vary according to the size of your swing. For a full swing, your stance is no narrower than your hips and no wider than your shoulders. Another tip relates to the length of your club: the shorter your club, the narrower the width of your stance.

Only now do you slightly flex your knees. It's a small flex; make sure that you can still see your shoelaces when you look down. If you flex your knees before making your bend, you'll bend

Fig. 5. Add a slight knee bend, and you have a correct setup.

Fig. 6. Flexing the knees too much puts your weight on your heels and straightens your spine. As a result, you won't have room to swing your arms.

incorrectly—from the waist. Allow your arms to hang straight down from your shoulders so you have lots of room in which to swing them, (see figure 5). If you flex your knees too much, you won't have enough room to swing your arms, as shown in figure 6. At the correct address position, your weight is equally distributed on both feet.

Here's a drill for getting the feel of your upper-body, or torso, and hip positions. Stand with your left shoulder perpendicular to a full-length mirror. Cross your arms in front of your chest and turn toward the mirror so that your belt buckle, hips, and torso are facing it. As you turn, your

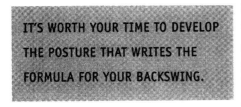

IT'S WORTH YOUR TIME TO DEVELOP THE POSTURE THAT WRITES THE FORMULA FOR YOUR BACKSWING.

right knee comes over and "kisses" your left knee, shifting 90 percent of your weight into your left hip socket as you rotate. You're up on your right toe. If you tilt now, just a little bit, to your right side,

you'll feel what your correct **finish position** is like for your torso and hips. In this finish position, your right hip is tilted about 2 inches lower than your left hip.

Figure 7 illustrates three ball positions relative to the point on your left shoulder or logo on your shirt. PGA teaching professional Mike Adams taught me that relating the ball position to your torso is easier than adjusting it to where your feet are

Fig. 7. Three ball positions relative to the left shoulder or upper torso.

positioned. As shown, the ball position when you're using a **short iron** is to the left side of your face. The position for **mid-irons** and fairway woods is off the logo on your shirt. For a driver, the ball should be positioned off your left armpit.

Figure 8 illustrates the incorrect, and then the correct, **prehinge engagement.** This is the result of using the correct posture, with the proper angle between the clubshaft and your forearms. Practice this correct posture in a full-length mirror, using figure 8 as your guide.

Fig. 8.   Prehinge engagement, incorrect (left) and correct (right).

THE SWING

How do I teach new students to develop their swing? Let me say a little about the conceptualization behind Three-Shot Golf so these comments will be in context.

I teach consistent **shotmaking,** rather than going for distance, which can be elusive and frustrating for beginners and even for some of you advanced players. It's true that particular equipment, such as a longer clubshaft, can help the ball go farther. The loft of the club (the degree to which the clubface is angled upward) affects the trajectory or launch angle of the ball. Let your

A

B

Fig. 9. The hula hoop helps demonstrate the plane on which the club should move. A shows the correct inclined plane. B and C show the extremes of vertical and horizontal.

C

equipment do its part in helping you meet your distance goals. I encourage you to strive for consistency, hitting the ball solidly and advancing it with the *needed* distance and proper trajectory.

If women are to play great golf, an objective should be developing centeredness of hit—that is, making solid ball contact. For gaining respectable distance, centeredness of hit is more important than clubhead speed at impact. *It is centeredness of hit that produces the consistency of* **ball striking,** *which moves the ball along in play.*

In order to attain centeredness of hit or a solid golf shot, you must swing your clubshaft on an **inclined plane.** This must happen particularly on the downswing if you're to hit a solid, straight, effortless shot. I teach my students to understand the concept of the inclined plane by using a child's hula hoop. I hold the hula hoop on a plane that's not like that of a merry-go-round or a Ferris wheel, but more like a Tilt-a-Whirl. Look at figure 9 to see the differences among the too-vertical, or Ferris wheel swing shape; the too-rounded, or merry-go-round swing shape; and the properly inclined plane for your swing.

Swinging the clubshaft on this inclined plane means you'll be more likely to hit the ball correctly. When you learn to take the clubshaft back on the inclined plane on your **upswing,** you are more likely to follow through with your **downswing** on the inclined plane as well.

Okay. Now you have the basics. Let's learn the first of the Three Shots, the 30-yard pitch shot.

CHAPTER TWO

Shot #1–
The 30-Yard Pitch Shot

This important approach shot is my secret weapon. It can become yours, too, with a helpful instructor to make sure you've got this shot accurately lined up, and with a savvy practice plan. This pitch shot is what you need to get onto the green *every* time from 30, 40, or 50 yards out. I give my students the guarantee that if they master this shot, they will lower their scores and get the ball onto the green every time.

For you beginners, this pitch shot is a miniature swing from which you can develop your full swing. A miniature swing has a shorter backswing and downswing than are needed for a full swing. The through-motion is also considerably less in a miniature swing than in a full one. The miniature swing produces little clubhead speed and, therefore, less distance than a full swing. You must rely on the loft of your club to carry the ball in the desired path.

Getting this pitch shot is like learning to ski on the bunny slopes before you try to tackle the black-diamond runs with the moguls. Starting with this shot means that you can hit a very accurate golf shot on the first day you try.

Why do I emphasize this shot? First, I know that you'll be using a pitch shot from 50 yards and in on almost every hole. It just makes sense for a woman player to master a shot that will work for her. I've also observed that many women get mentally rattled near the greens. I want my students to have a shot that gives them confidence by giving them the means to get the ball onto the green consistently and reliably.

Second, I'm well aware that a woman who makes 30 putts in a round can end up with a final score of either 120 or 75. What's the difference? It's not her putting. It's all in the approach shots that get her to the green so she has the chance to putt. If you are a great putter but can't get onto the green, it'll be difficult to improve your score.

For you advanced players, this 30-yard lofted pitch shot doesn't require youth, strength, or clubhead speed to be successful. As you learn the proper setup and use my time-saving practice drills, you can rapidly learn to loft the ball onto the green every time, for consistent results. The goal is to make solid ball contact that takes the ball up in the air with the required trajectory. Yes, it's a shot that may need to go only 30 yards, but you can make it a great golf shot and improve your full swing from it, just as a beginner can learn a full swing by learning this miniature swing.

A pitch shot is a defined as a shot that spends more time in the air than on the ground. The result is more "fly" than roll. The **shape** of an ideal pitch shot, therefore, is maximum time in the air and minimum time on the ground. With the pitch shot, you get the ball into the air to send it up and over something—a mound, a sand trap, or tall grass—or onto an elevated green. If you're thinking, "I've got to get this ball in the air because of this particular obstacle," you should use a pitch shot.

You also use a pitch shot in some cases when there isn't an obvious obstacle like a bunker or an elevated green. For example, you pitch when you can't roll the ball through the grass because it's too tall, too damp, or too soft. The ground's surface may be too bumpy to roll the ball through. I recommend the pitch shot at those times when I've seen women be tempted to roll the ball over 30 yards with a 7-iron.

I can understand why they want to do this, and it would be great if it worked. I'm just aware from my experience as a tour player that you often don't know for certain what the surface of the ground is like. The fairway surface is not smooth and reliable like the green. The pitch shot thus comes in handy to get over stretches of uncertain surface.

The distance of a pitch shot is determined by the size of your swing, which in this case is a miniature swing. The size of your swing is, in turn, determined by your setup. There are specific things you can do to make your swing on this pitch shot smaller. You won't be **addressing** the ball like you will later with a full swing, for instance. Instead, this is a lower-body-oriented golf shot with a slight wrist hinge and some arm swing. For this shot you should use a lofted club, either a pitching wedge, a sand wedge, or even the fashionable lob wedge. This is a relatively new piece of equipment that now comprises one-third of the three-wedge system in the golf bag. Before, people used a two-wedge system. Each of these three wedges has a particular degree of loft. The pitching wedge lofts the ball to some degree, while the sand wedge causes it to fly higher into the air. The lob wedge has the highest trajectory.

The pitching wedge is more appropriate to use than the sand wedge when the distance is greater. You can hit your pitching wedge 60 yards. The pitching wedge is also more helpful for shots that are uphill; when your approach shot is downhill, use your sand wedge. And the pitching wedge works better than the sand wedge when you need the ball to roll a little more on the ground.

With its greater loft, the sand wedge has a higher launch angle than the pitching wedge. This means that a ball hit with your sand wedge stops rolling more quickly when it lands on the green. You can use the sand wedge to hit 50 yards. The lob wedge can be used for a 30-yard, high-trajectory shot for elevated greens. Also note that you can take a full swing with a lob wedge to achieve greater clubhead speed at impact; as a result, the ball will go higher.

It's important for me to mention here that there are only a couple of ways to stop the ball on the green: with spin and with trajectory. A ball falling straight out of the sky with no spin will stop on the green. Obviously, a ball coming onto a green with a lower trajectory (that is, coming in at an angle) and no backspin will roll forward.

Achieving backspin is a more advanced skill and something to consider working on as you progress. However, you can certainly get trajectory—hitting the ball high into the air and having it come down toward the flagstick—by using the lob wedge. And this way you don't need to have a well-developed backspin to get the ball to fly the way you want it to.

1 PITCH-SHOT SETUP

To set up for a pitch shot, you need to grip down to the middle of the grip. The setup on this shot requires a stance that is narrower than the width of your hips and also **open**. You open your stance by dropping your left foot back to the arch of your right foot and slightly flaring your left toe.

Ball position plays an important role in pitching. The ball must be placed in the center of your stance. You also want to set up so that on your swing, you'll hit the ball before you hit the ground, with an arc whose bottom falls in front of the ball. To do this, start with your weight resting slightly more in your left hip socket. If you were to put a scale under each foot while you stood in such a stance, you'd find 60 percent of your weight on your left side and 40 percent on your right. This weight differential should remain throughout your swing; there will be no weight transfer as you make your shot. (I'll discuss your actual shot mechanics below.)

This setup—with the ball centered, your weight more on your left side, and your hands and sternum slightly ahead of the ball—will assist you in creating an ideal pitch shot.

1 POWER GENERATORS IN THE GOLF SWING

Three power generators are used in golf. **Arm swing** is the first of the three power generators in golf. Every golf motion has an arm swing, from a full swing to a putt. The wrist hinge is the second power generator, and I'll say more about this one later in the chapter.

The **pivot,** or motion of the body, is the third power generator and the least influential of the three. When the arms swing, the body pivots. It's helpful to think of the body as consisting of two parts—the upper body and the lower body. In a golf swing, the upper and lower body do not turn the same amount. There is a separation in the pivot; the upper body turns separately from the lower body.

The upper body, or torso, turns 90 degrees to the target line on the backswing, and the lower body turns 45 degrees. This difference in the amount that the upper and lower bodies pivot around the spine produces a coiling action of the body. You can see this dramatically displayed in the swings of golfers like Tiger Woods, Patty Sheehan, Beth Daniels, John Daly, and Si Re Pak.

The backswing is an upper-body-oriented motion. At the top of the backswing, your upper body is rotated farther around than your lower body. You start your downswing by moving your lower body to produce the coil.

A

Fig. 10 The pitch shot, from the top of the backswing to the follow-through.

While we're discussing pivot, let me say a little about the **width** of your golf swing. This refers to the distance your hands are from your chest. As you move through the backswing and then on to your downswing, you want to make certain that this distance doesn't change. If your swing width *is* differ-ent from the backswing to the downswing because you don't pivot, you'll have to make an adjustment. For example, if on your backswing you don't rotate your body and your arms come in close to you, this will cause the width of the swing to become narrower. You will top the ball. The golf swing therefore becomes a "push" motion

B

C   D

to you instead of a swing. Your arms come toward you on the back-swing and then out on the downswing.

The width of my golf swing does not change. My hands are the same distance from my chest throughout my backswing and all the way down to the point of impact. (On my **forward swing,** however, my arms have become extended and the distance is greater.)

When a woman player has trouble with this, it's because her grip is too tight for the wrist hinge to occur, and because she isn't pivoting properly. I work with my students to help them keep the width of their swing the same during the backswing and down to the point of impact.

This pitch shot includes some **lower-body motion** and it's very important that you understand the way that it works. In the pitch shot, you aren't driving your hips to get the ball going. Examine figure 10A: On my backswing, my left hip pocket moves around to the right about 1 inch. On my forward swing, however, my left hip pocket moves about 6 inches, as illustrated in figure 10B.

In the motion of the golf swing, it's important that your arms be supported and stabilized with your body. The body motion doesn't drive the arms. You can't drive the body. You have to swing your arms in sequence with your body motion. If your arms get too far behind your body motion, your body will feel over-rotated. Your arms may feel like they're waving as they move past the ball.

It's important that when you swing the club, your arms stay in front of your body. Your hips definitely move farther on the forward swing than they do in the backswing of the pitch shot (although not with the energy you use in the full swing)—but the arms always go first, as in figures 10C and 10D.

The lower body "moves through," making room for the arms to swing on the follow-through and extend through the shot. It's important that your arms stay in front of you in golf. The fact that your body pivots and your wrists hinge allows the club to swing around you in an arc. If you don't move your lower body on the backswing and don't continue this pivot on the follow-through, you lose the effect of the arm swing as a power generator. What happens is that your arms will extend before you get to the ball and you'll hit the ball **fat,** meaning that you strike the ground before your club hits the ball. Or you'll stand up to make room and **top** the ball, meaning that you have struck it on or above its equator or midpoint.

In both a miniature and a full swing, there's a slight wrist hinge that results naturally as your arms swing. As I noted earlier, this slight hinging action is the third power generator; it helps initiate the proper **arc** and gets the club into the air, as in figure 11. The wrist hinge is formed when your extended left forearm and the clubshaft make a right angle. This hinging action should happen when your forearm is level to the ground on the backswing.

This happens gradually and continuously on the backswing. It puts some energy into the clubshaft.

I remind my students that the only hinge on the backswing is with the left wrist. This hinging action starts on the backswing. As your arms swing around and up and your body pivots, both wrists gradually hinge. I demonstrate for my students the correct grip and that the hands must be soft enough on the club to allow this wrist

A   **B**

Fig. 11. A slight wrist hinge is one of the power generators for the pitch and other shots that require a swing motion.

hinge to occur. I have them practice deliberately maintaining the hinge on the downswing.

Ironically, a lot of new women golfers don't feel comfortable allowing their wrists to hinge. They comment that it feels like they're losing control of the clubhead. When they keep their wrists stiff and make an arm swing along with a little bit of body motion, they do see some results: They hit the ball straight. But they're missing out on gaining what could be considerable distance, because their stiff wrists prevent them from attaining the clubhead speed that produces distance. The wrist hinge, done while you swing on the inclined plane that I discussed in chapter 1, creates leverage and is the number one power producer.

In my clinics I demonstrate the importance of the wrist hinge and inclined plane by hitting golf balls while seated in a chair placed out by the tees. Obviously, when I'm seated I've eliminated the power generator of lower-body motion. Students can see their potential for attaining distance when I hit balls 180 yards with my 3-wood while seated.

Now try a drill called the underarm toss; this will enable you to feel the correct clubface orientation and the direction in which the ball should travel. Figure 12 demonstrates how to swing your right arm under your left. This drill will show you how to move your body, particularly your lower body, in relation to your arm swing when you swing the club toward the ball.

It'll help you see how to execute the miniature arm swing necessary for the pitch shot, which has less backswing and forward swing than a full swing. It'll also help you master the lower third of your golf swing—the final 2 inches before your club strikes the ball. Practicing this drill should help you realize that even when your swing is a small one, it doesn't mean that you don't use your body. Whenever your arms swing outside the width of your body, you have to start pivoting to keep your arms swinging in an arc.

The underarm toss teaches you the importance of the pivot in your arm swing. You're learning to avoid the top shot. You're also learning to find the bottom of your swing's arc consistently, every time. Remember, though, that this is an underarm *toss*, not an underhand flick. You need to keep the clubhead under your hands so that you don't flick or scoop the ball with your wrists. You're trying to hit the ball down into the ground so that it'll fly up.

There isn't as much wrist hinge on the pitch as there is on a full swing. In this underhanded toss, you'll find that the majority of your weight is on your left side. You'll notice that your right shoulder always works under—not down, but *under*—your left shoulder. People top the ball when their right shoulders work over the top of their left shoulders. It should feel as if you're brushing the grass with your right shoulder, always working under as your torso and lower body rotate and support your swinging arms.

Fig. 12. The ball-toss drill will help you get a feel for the correct way your lower body should move in relation to your arm swing throughout the pitching motion. Take your 5-iron and stand it vertically to the ground, with the club-head on the ground. Place your left hand facing down on the top of the club handle. With the ball in your right hand, toss the ball by swinging your right arm under your left arm. The key is to make sure you move your lower body in sequence with the arm swing.

This drill forces your lower body and your arm swing to move in sequence while restricting and positioning your upper body so that it doesn't over-rotate or come over the top of your motion. Remember, the pitch shot is a lower-body-oriented motion. If your lower body stops and your arms don't have room to swing through, you'll turn this swing into an underhanded wrist flick.

It's also important to maintain your spine angle as you rotate through this motion. Don't change your **spine elevation**—that is, don't stand up or come out of your correct posture as you rotate through.

Here's a tip I give students learning this mini swing: At the finish position, your spine should be tilted so that the buttons on your shirt are tilted in the manner shown in figure 13.

Look at figure 14. Here you see that I'm not moving my arms in sequence with my lower body. The result is a top shot, one in which you've run out of room for your arms to swing through, and a resulting ball trajectory that *isn't* in the air.

I show my beginning students how the arms swing up and then fall down in a pitch shot. After the arms swing up,

Fig. 13. At the top of the backswing, the spine is tilted and the sternum is still over the spot where the ball lay.

they must fall because of the force of gravity. You don't have to expend effort to put a lot of force on the ball at impact. The size of your arm swing, plus gravity pulling down on the weight of your arms and club, is enough.

As your arms fall down and you hit the ball down into the ground, the ball pops up. This is important, because the pitch shot needs to get up in the air. The way to get the ball into the air is to hit down on it. A pitch shot is thus a slightly descending blow, as seen in figure 15. Hard as it is to imagine, that's what the shot is really doing. When you strike simultaneously the ball and the bottom of the arc—the ground— your ball will go up into the air. A properly executed pitch shot will take a slight **divot,** a little section of turf torn up by your clubhead. It's a good sign. Do remember to repair the divot by placing the bit of turf gently back into place before you move on.

If you aren't taking divots, you may well be topping the ball. To correct such a topping motion, try this drill. Take some tees and stick them down into the turf so they are just level with the surface of

Fig. 14. Doing the ball-toss drill incorrectly— the ball moves with far less momentum because the lower body has not turned in sequence with the arms. If the lower body stops moving through, this limits the amount of room for the arms to swing.

the ground. Try your pitch shot and see if you can dig the tee and a divot out of the ground with your club. If you can't, you're still topping the ball. You'll need to work more on the technique of allowing the club to fall down into the ground. Avoid trying to hit the ball into the air with a scooping (wrist-flick) motion. This causes a top shot.

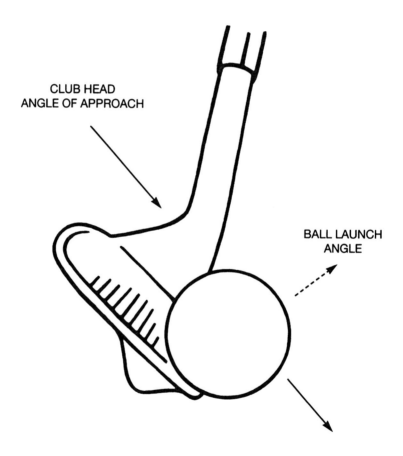

Fig. 15. The slightly descending blow of the pitch shot.

Sometimes I have a new student who attempts to make a big weight transfer during her miniature swing. Basically, with the pitch shot, there isn't time for that. I'll see her attempt the weight transfer but then bottom out early and hit behind the ball. And occasionally a new student will need correction on her pitch shot because she's already had the experience of hitting behind the ball, resulting from trying to shift her weight too much. I see her swinging her arms in too closely to avoid hitting behind the ball—but she tops it instead.

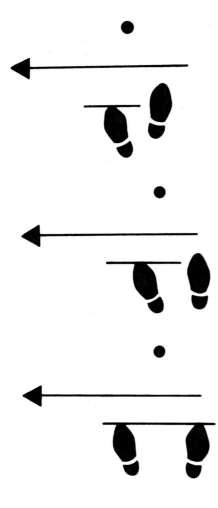

As I noted earlier, when you stop your lower-body motion too early, your arms extend too early in the swing (that is, you get to the bottom of the arc too early in the swing). The result is that you hit the ground or feel the need to "stand up." The result will be a top shot.

I've mentioned that a pitch shot can range from 30 to 50 yards, depending on the distance you need to carry the ball. So how do you change the range of your pitch shot? The distance of your shot will be

Fig. 16. Changing your setup to alter the distance of your pitch shot.

directly affected by the size of your arm swing. And the size of your arm swing changes with modifications in your setup: how far down you grip the club, how wide your stance is, and how much you flare your left toe.

Still, for all pitch shots of between 30 and 50 yards, the ball position is centered, your hands are centered in front of your sternum, and the butt of your club points toward the center of your body. Figure 16 shows you how to change the setup to alter the distance of your pitch shot.

I have a story to share with you about learning distance control in my pitch shot. It happened back in my tour days, after I'd been touring for about four years. I could hit a wedge shot, but I didn't know how to control my distance. So I spent an entire winter working on nothing but wedge shots. That was my goal—to learn wedge shots of 60, 70, or 80 yards. What I did was pace off 50 yards on the driving range and put a towel on the ground. Then I'd pace off another 10 yards and drop another towel. I'd pace off 10 more yards, and down went another towel.

I hit thousands of shots to those towels, learning the difference between 60 yards and 70, and 70 yards and 80. I got so I could land the ball exactly the distance I wanted. I had developed into a very good wedge player who had the distance control I'd wanted. I actually wore out a wedge that winter because I practiced at the Carmel Valley Ranch, whose driving range had a very sandy base. When I went back on tour the next season, I was very confident about my wedge play.

I know that most women don't have the hours to spend practicing that I did. I share this with you to remind you that things in golf get much better with repetition—with repeatedly practicing something correctly. Practice is where confidence starts.

What about when you are inside 30 yards—do you know when to use your pitch shot then? The answer is to look at your shot and ask yourself, "Do I want this ball to land and stop on the green, or do I want it to land and roll?" If you want the ball to land

and stop, then you need a pitch shot. What you're seeing is that you need some trajectory to lift the ball up and over; then it should hit and stop, because there's no room for it to roll.

If you assess the shot and decide that the ball should land and roll, then you should make more of a "bump-and-run" shot, with a little different setup. You won't use the power generators here, except for a moderate arm swing. The weight of your body should start, stay, and finish on your left side. Use your pitching wedge or 9-iron and place your ball a little farther back in your stance—off your right toe—as you would for a chip shot (which I'll describe in chapter 5).

Let me reiterate why this pitch shot is so important. In order to become a bogey golfer, one who shoots around 90, *you have to get your approach shots onto the green.* You can be the best putter in the world; if you can't get onto the green, though, you'll struggle to score. One-putting for an 8 is going to discourage you and interfere with your improvement. You have to get onto the green consistently, and you use the pitch shot to accomplish this.

When I was a little kid, the first thing my professional, Fred Wetmore, taught me was a pitch shot. I was only eight years old at the time and lived in a little town near Carmel. He was a great guy who let us kids stripe the range balls (you had to do it yourself back then), and pick up all the balls at the end of the day. He'd give us a milk shake or hot dog for helping. In my neighborhood, many of the kids played golf because of Fred. I was one of the few girls who loved golf.

Every day I was at the range first thing in the morning. Fred would hand me a bucket of balls and tell me to hit pitch shots. In fact, he placed me 10 yards behind a low tree branch—maybe 6 feet off the ground—and had me hit my pitching wedge. "Go hit low wedge shots under that tree. Don't put the ball back in your stance," were his instructions.

This was a very difficult shot. I spent many months hitting balls off the tree. For a long time I didn't hit any shots correctly;

I'd get so frustrated. Fred just kept handing me the bucket of balls and telling me to use my pitching wedge. Although I didn't want to do it and it wasn't clear to me what he was trying to teach me, I did as he instructed because I trusted him. When I finished each bucket all he'd say was, "That's fine."

Yes, it was incredibly frustrating spending all those days practicing a miniature swing. But eventually I could a hit pitch shot better than just about anybody. I could hit a great low pitch shot, and a great high pitching wedge shot. I could put spin on any pitch shot. Fred had taught me how to make solid ball contact at the age of eight.

I became a very good player pretty quickly, given Fred's wise mentoring. The first time I played nine holes, at eight, I shot 45. Fred had deliberately taught me about the most important part of a golf swing—the bottom 2 inches, "impact," where the bottom of the swing's arc is. I learned what it felt like when the club met the ball correctly—the feel of a good golf shot. Only *after* I knew how to get solid ball contact did he teach me how to hit for distance.

I must say that I didn't like the drills at the time, but they taught me the benefits of sticking with something, and how to remain persistent, and which shot was the one to learn first. That's why the pitch became the core of Three-Shot Golf—because it worked so well for me. And I have seen how well it works for my students. It can work for you, too.

The pitch is a great shot to have in your bag of tricks if you're struggling with your full swing—or indeed, if you find yourself

I KNOW IT'S DIFFICULT TO WORK ON A LITTLE SHOT LIKE THIS PITCH WHEN IT SEEMS LIKE GOLF IS MADE UP OF FULL-SWING SHOTS. BUT GOING AFTER A BIG SWING TOO SOON IS LIKE TRYING TO LEARN TO SKI ON THE BLACK-DIAMOND RUNS WITH BIG MOGULS INSTEAD OF FIRST GETTING GOOD ON THE BUNNY SLOPES.

frustrated at almost any point in your learning process. Let's say you're having trouble hitting the ball straight—that ball contact is not solid with your full-swing shots. This pitch shot is helpful to return to because you can make your shot swing smaller, take away some of the swing motion, and thus get solid ball contact back. You can get your confidence going again and gradually return to your full swing.

I tell my students that when they're struggling, they'll be better off not sticking with the big-swing motions but instead switching back to practicing this miniature swing. I don't want them struggling when they are hitting the ball badly. Instead, I instruct them to stop practicing mistakes and switch back to the miniature swing, the pitch shot, to regain their confidence and get some results.

Mastering the pitch shot teaches you what impact feels like, and what your body feels like when you strike the ball and make solid ball contact. You're going to use this pitch shot to avoid double bogeys, especially when the ball is sitting right in front of the green. By mastering this pitch shot, you can always approach the green and save bogey. Remember—*this shot is a stroke saver*. With your instructor's help and my tips, you can master this mini swing and get onto the green every time.

CHAPTER THREE

Shot #2– Fairway Wood Heaven

One of the two advancement shots that are important for women is the fairway wood shot. It's a full-swing shot that develops from the miniature swing you used for your pitch. Recall that this miniature swing involves the lower third of the swing, the 2 inches that are at the bottom of the swing's arc.

To make an efficient transition to fairway woods, start with your pitch shot as you learned it in chapter 2, and then begin to hit these pitch shots with your 7-iron. Concentrate on solid ball contact every time—as you did with the pitch shot—and on finding the bottom of the arc as you swing, allowing your arms to fall, and creating a slight descending blow. Then make this swing a bit larger, up to a three-quarters swing, while still making good ball contact. Then in gradual, transitional steps, build up to a full

47

swing. Make a full-swing motion with the iron you like best, then switch to your fairway wood.

I often find that my students want to get to this full swing right away, before they have achieved solid ball contact with the miniature swing. Their impatience is understandable. (If I could give my students one thing it would be patience!) But my experience has shown me that mastering the lower one-third of the arc of a full swing before progressing will give you much better results as you begin to develop and refine your full swing. For those of you seasoned players frustrated with your full swing, you too may find it helpful to go back to the miniature swing and get some really good pitch shots going. Then, with your instructor, return to your full swing. I bet you'll find it easier to hit.

I see happier faces when my students have achieved solid ball contact in a lesson because it *feels* like good golf. Hitting one ball really far—perhaps by accident as much as anything else—just doesn't feel this way.

Most women need to spend more time on the fairway wood full-swing shot than on iron shots. However, before you begin to make a full swing, find one of those mid-irons that you really like—a 6- or 7-iron, maybe—and make the transition from a pitch shot to a full golf swing with this iron. You'll increase your chances of getting comfortable with the fairway wood shots if you first make a full swing and achieve some success with this iron.

> REMEMBER HOW EXHILARATING IT WAS AS A KID TO RIDE YOUR BIKE WITHOUT THOSE TRAINING WHEELS? MOVE THE BALL OFF THE TEE SOON AND TRY SWINGING OFF THE GRASS!

Switch to the fairway wood as soon as you get results. Get your pitch shot down first, make this miniature swing bigger using your favorite iron, then move *quickly* into your fairway wood shots, because you'll be making a lot of them. To learn golf quickly, you

Fig. 17. Ball position changes as your club selection changes. Play your woods with the ball off your left armpit.

need this fairway wood shot *soon*. If you linger too long making short iron shots, it's going to be a little scary when you suddenly find yourself with a much longer club in your hands.

The key to fairway wood heaven is to start by doing most of your practicing with fairway 5- or 7-woods off a tee. A teed ball is easier to hit, because you don't have to move it off the ground; it's already off the ground. As soon as you gain some confidence, switch to hitting these shots off the grass. Taking the tee away once you get the feel of this shot is like taking the training wheels off a bike. Go after it!

The key to playing bogey golf is to hit *solid* golf shots. If you're hitting the ball solidly with the right trajectory, you're going to be advancing the ball the best you can with the swing that you have. If you're struggling with ball contact, go back to the pitch shot to get the feeling of a solid golf shot.

YOU CAN PLAY BOGEY GOLF WHEN YOU CAN HIT A SHOT 110 YARDS OFF THE GRASS AND HAVE DEVELOPED YOUR SHORTER SHOTS.

My idea of fairway wood heaven is to hit a 110-yard shot, carried into the air, off the grass. That's the reasonable and attainable distance goal we're going after. The grip for this shot is the overlapping grip taught in chapter 1. The setup is also similar—with a few modifications, noted below.

For the fairway wood shot you use basically the same swing as for your mini or pitch shot, but add more upswing and downswing with your arms and more torso rotation on the backswing, making this a **full swing.** In the setup you move the ball forward in your stance, positioning it off your left armpit (as in figure 17). Pick your favorite fairway wood, your 5-, 7-, or maybe your 9-wood. In this shot you allow the club to "sweep," brushing the top of the grass. You don't want to dig at the ball.

Before, with the pitch shot, you were standing fairly close to the ball holding your pitching wedge, which is one of the shorter clubs in your bag. Now, with the fairway wood shot, you stand farther away from the ball, so that more of your clubshaft needs to swing like a Tilt-a-Whirl around your torso. Your clubshaft needs to be on an inclined plane—especially on your downswing.

The shaft swings at a right angle to your spine, but it swings on an inclined plane relative to the ground. You can think of swinging the golf club, theoretically, perpendicularly to your spine, around it. If you've ever played baseball and had someone pitch a ball to you—a low outside pitch to the plate—and you had to hit it into left field, that's what a golf shot is. You've got to bend down to get the ball in golf, just like you do in baseball.

When you swing on this inclined plane, your hands should feel like they're coming toward your right shoulder on the backswing; on your follow-through your hands should feel like they're coming toward your left shoulder. In other words, your hands swing through from your right shoulder to your left as you swing in this arc.

It's much the same in baseball. If you stand straight up with your spine vertical to the ground and swing the bat horizontally to the

A

B

Fig. 18. The inclined plane of the fairway wood, halfway through the backswing (A), and at the top of the backswing (B).

ground, it'll feel like your hands go from your right shoulder, as they swing the bat, to your left shoulder as you (hopefully) hit a home run. The right shoulder *always* works slightly under (not down) as you swing through.

It's the same motion in golf. You tilt over. Your hands swing through from your right shoulder to your left. That's golf.

If your swing has a tendency to be vertical to the ground—more like a Ferris wheel than a Tilt-a-Whirl—you'll struggle with your fairway woods. You've got to get the clubshaft swinging more on the inclined plane. If you do okay with your short irons, for instance, but have trouble with the longer fairway woods, it's because you're not swinging on enough of an inclined plane. Take the path or plane of your swing and tilt it more toward you.

In a fairway wood shot your arms will go in and up, causing greater rotation of your torso. A greater wrist hinge is produced automatically by gravity when you swing in this full arc. The importance of having your club on an inclined plane will become very clear as you begin to swing a longer club. The inclined plane of this sweep will feel more like it *surrounds* you, and you'll have a shallower angle of approach, as in figure 18.

Here are some physical truisms that I teach my students. You can swing your arms and not move your body—but only for the width of your body. As soon as your arms swing outside the width of your body you must rotate one way, in the direction you're swinging your arms, and then the other. In a golf swing, when you rotate on the upswing you don't rotate very far. Your hips turn on the upswing only 2 or 3 inches.

But on my downswing, my left hip pocket turns all the way around behind me—maybe 5 inches. Therefore, the energy moving in that direction on the downswing has to be greater. You don't "drive" your hips, but you need to rotate them fully through.

You must come down on an inclined plane to hit a good fairway wood shot, as shown in figures 19 and 20. The finish shot position for fairway woods is shown in figure 21.

YOU MAY HAVE HEARD FROM OTHER INSTRUCTORS, "DRIVE YOUR HIPS; DRIVE YOUR LEGS." BUT I DON'T HIT THE BALL WITH MY LEGS. I HIT THE BALL WITH MY *CLUB*. THE HIPS, LEGS, AND LOWER BODY SUPPORT AND ROTATE; THEY DON'T DRIVE.

With full-swing shots like the fairway wood shot you stand, as I've mentioned, farther away from the ball. And the farther you stand away from the ball, the greater will be the need to swing on an inclined plane. A vertical swing path won't work. If you do swing

Fig. 19. Fairway wood shot at impact . . .

Fig. 20. . . . and at follow-through. Note that the inclined plane remains constant and the club shaft is following this path.

Fig. 21. The clubshaft is still on the inclined plane even at the finish of the swing.

the clubshaft too vertically on a full swing, the club will come into the ball too steeply (straight down), causing a pop-up shot or **slice.**

People often struggle as they're learning to play golf because of the beginner's tendency to have a very vertical downswing. When your club is coming down too vertically—especially a long club—it's very difficult to hit a solid golf shot. The club is actually *swinging at you in* a vertical swing path, which is why you'll see people "standing up" to get out of the way and then topping their golf balls. This error is illustrated in figure 22.

Unfortunately, most golfers shooting 100 or greater have a tendency to slice the ball on fairway wood shots, meaning that they hit their shots starting to the left of the target line and finishing to the right of it. Another way to understand a slice is this: When you slice

Fig. 22. If your clubshaft follows too vertical a plane, as here, the result is a slice.

the ball, you are not swinging on an inclined plane and, therefore, you are hitting on the outside of the golf ball. Figure 23 illustrates this. In comparison, when you're closer to the ball with a shorter club for a pitch shot, you can get away with a more vertical swing path. To help my students stop swinging in too vertical a swing path on fairway wood shots, I have them check to see if their torso and shoulders are turning 90 degrees to the target line on the backswing.

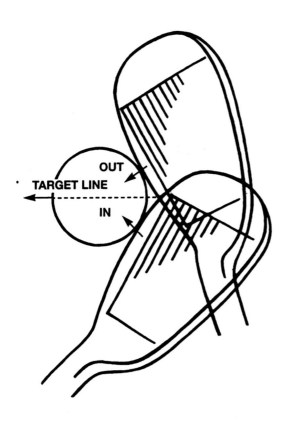

Fig. 23. Hitting the outside of the ball, from swinging in a vertical plane, yields a slice. Swing on an inclined plane and you will hit the inside of the ball, automatically resulting in a straight shot.

Here's an exercise that may help those of you who are kinesthetic learners (people who seem to learn best by "feel") to acquire the *feeling* of swinging on an inclined plane. Imagine that at the top of your backswing, you are balancing with your dominant hand a small round tray with a tall glass of water on it. Now imagine that while initiating your downswing, you have to keep the glass upright on the tray. Without having the correct feeling for the inclined plane, most people will dump the glass and its contents instantly as they transfer from the backswing to the downswing.

If you can feel how your hand turns to keep the glass balanced on the tray at the very beginning of the transition from backswing to downswing, you'll be learning how to move the clubshaft on an inclined plane. Take a look at figure 24; the glass stays on the tray for the initial part of the downswing, because the golfer is moving her right hand down along the inclined plane. This exercise gives you a kinesthetic hint at how you want to move your clubshaft.

With a fairway wood shot, you have to swing on an inclined plane in order to hit the ball into the air. I tell my students that

Fig. 24. Use this mental image to help get the right inclined plane. At the top of your backswing, imagine you are holding a glass of water on a tray in your right hand. As your downswing begins, you should keep the glass on the tray.

the fairway wood shot is more of an "around" swing, like the Tilt-a-Whirl. If you tend to have a swing more like a Ferris wheel—meaning too steep—then the farther you stand from the ball (as longer clubs force you to do), the more you will struggle to get your clubshaft to move on the inclined plane. Consequently, you'll probably slice the ball and lose distance.

What do I recommend when a student comes to me with a dramatic slice? First, I ask her what she thinks causes a slice. A lot of times she'll say it's due to her weight transfer.

I listen carefully, and then ask her to visualize what I'm talking about as I explain the two parts of the golf swing. First, I describe the way the body supports the golf club—stabilizing and rotating it—along with the arm swing, and how the arms swing the club in and up. Then, I talk about the second part of the swing as relating to the golf club—the instrument itself—and how it's swinging.

I next tell her to make a correction to her slice by concentrating only on the golf club itself, how the clubshaft swings in its arc, and to refrain from thinking about her body's motion or her arm swing. In a slice her arc would be "outside in," meaning that she'd hit too much on the outside of the golf ball.

I show her that, in a slice, the clubshaft is swinging too vertically to the ground and not enough on the inclined plane. A golfer who slices swings in this too-vertical way, which starts the golf ball to the left of the target line and spins it back to the right. This shot loses distance. She may have been given a fix by her instructor, who told her to try to hit the "inside" of the golf ball. I find it is much clearer for my students if I can get them to understand that they will not hit the dreaded slice if they swing the clubshaft on an inclined plane. I tell them that they must establish the inclined plane on the backswing, and then must stay on this plane on the downswing. By doing this, they will properly hit the inside of the golf ball, without having to think consciously about hitting inside or outside.

In my explanation I demonstrate how the golf club must swing on an inclined plane with pictures, on video, and in a mirror to help each student experience what this will feel like done correctly. The feeling of the golf club and her body will be *strong* when she swings her club on the inclined plane, I tell her.

Slicers should remember that the body must rotate and support the swing. Many people don't get their arms to move correctly to get the clubshaft onto an inclined plane. I work with these students on their pivots. I want to make certain that each student's shoulders are turned 90 degrees to the target line on her backswing. If her shoulders are under-rotated on the backswing, then her arm swing overall won't be sufficiently large-around enough to get the club to move on an inclined plane, likely causing a slice.

The correct pivot allows the arms to swing and the wrists to hinge properly, so that the club can move on an inclined plane. Then hitting a straight shot is much likelier.

When you swing on the inclined plane, you will feel this same sense of your club and body being strong *because of the leverage generated by the correct arm swing and wrist hinge*. It's important that when you hinge your wrists, the clubshaft stays on the inclined plane. In contrast, as soon as you swing the club on a vertical plane, you feel a loss of power. (Technically speaking, you lose leverage.)

When you observe a good player's swing, it looks like he or she isn't trying. It looks effortless. In a sense this is true, because that player is using the power generators correctly and swinging the shaft of the golf club on an inclined plane. As you learn to swing your club on this plane and effectively use your power generators, your swing will feel effortless, too.

1 PRESHOT ROUTINE

Now that you have your first full-swing shot, let me share my **preshot routine** with you. This is the routine you follow before making every shot. By definition, a *routine* is a set of habits that you don't need to think about. Practice your preshot routine so it becomes a habit—so it goes "underground," without the need for conscious thought. Mine is brief, but each step counts.

Step 1. **Select the right club** after determining the distance you want the ball to travel.

Step 2. **Pick your target and determine the shape of your shot.** You may find it helpful to come up from behind the ball, keeping it between you and the target. Say to yourself, "This is where I want to go." Draw an imaginary line from you through the ball to the target (as shown in figure 25). Come around and face that line as if it were a wall that squares up your feet, knees, hips, shoulders, and eyes. Place the club down behind the ball as if it's aiming right down that target line.

Step 3. **Aim** your sweet spot (the center of the clubface) at the target.

Step 4. **Align your body.** Your body should be facing the target line (the wall); make certain that your feet, knees, hips, shoulders, and eyes are all aligned with the target line.

Step 5. **Get the "waggle" (the feel) of your clubhead.** This concept was originated by Jim Flick. I do this by just getting the "waggle sense" in my hands before I swing. The waggle helps you in several ways. First, it's a way to release a little of any tension or stiffness you may have in your hands, the result of inexperience and too tight a grip. The waggling motion of your wrists also keeps your hands in place but allows the clubhead to be in motion. And you can use the waggle to set the pace for your swing, rapid or slow.

Step 6. **Rehearse the feel of the swing** by taking a practice swing at about half speed. Using half the actual speed keeps you from tiring yourself out, and saves time. Always rehearse a shot, even a pitch shot or any other that's not a full swing. This will give a feel for how big your swing should be. You want to feel the distance of these shorter shots—as well as full-swing shots.

Step 7. **Smile and go SWING.**

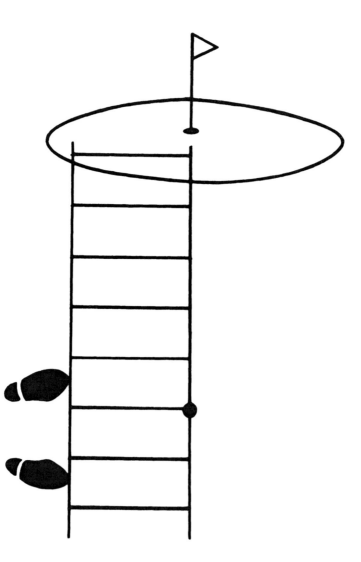

Fig. 25. The target line creates a "wall" that squares up your feet, knees, thighs, hips, shoulders, and eyes.

CHAPTER FOUR

Shot #3 –
The Impressive Tee Shot

The tee shot is the third element in three-shot golf. After they develop their shorter shots, I want my students to be able to hit a 7-wood 110 yards off a tee. Then they can really go out and play golf. My goal for my students with the tee shot is for them to become skillful enough that they can get off the first tee smartly and establish a sense of confidence from the very outset of a round.

The tee shot is often neglected by women players. This is probably because instructors know that the driver will accentuate any problem a student is having with her golf swing. If a student is slicing her drivers dramatically from left to right, she will have a slice with every club. But with the short irons, the slice won't be as observable. The longer the club, the more accentuated any swing problem becomes. So as an instructor, I'll have a student hit many short iron shots, because the loft in these shots straightens out the ball and helps her reduce her anxiety. It's a recipe for a nightmare when a novice arrives at a lesson with only her driver and says, "I just want to work with my driver."

A golf swing is a golf swing. If there's a problem that's causing a student anxiety, it's better to put a 7-iron in her hands. However, if she's getting results, I suggest that she "work up into her bag." This means going to the 6-iron, then the 7-wood, then the 3-wood off the tee. Then get out the driver. The driver will accentuate any problem in your swing, so work those problems out first with the more lofted clubs then get the 3-wood or driver into the lesson as soon as possible.

You want to get the drive to work for you, because the tee shot is one you will use on almost every hole.

First shop around and find a driver you're comfortable with. I recommend one with a 12-degree loft and flexible shaft. When you step up to that tee, I want you to have a driver you love in your hand—one with the right flex and loft, with a graphite shaft and titanium head, and with the shaft length that'll help you get distance. Let your professional help you with this decision.

If you haven't found a driver you love or if your improvement has been slower than you'd like, "bench" the club for a while and switch to one with a little more loft, like a 3-wood or even a 5-wood, and practice with that. However, keep in mind that the ball will go farther with your driver. You'll definitely want to get that club back into your bag as soon as possible.

Remember that the ball is positioned off your left armpit when use your driver. You're also standing farther away from the ball, so your posture will be slightly more vertical, but otherwise should feel the same. The driver is your lightest club, so use light grip pressure. This will allow for the considerable wrist hinge that's so important in this full swing. The wrist hinge, which allows leverage to occur, is the key to producing distance.

As with your fairway wood shot, you build off your mini swing to achieve the full swing of the tee shot. For the drive, the ball is already teed up, so you need not a descending blow but an ascending one to generate the desired trajectory. In other words, you don't have to hit down on the ball to get it to fly where you need it to, as in the pitch shot.

The proper setup helps you achieve this ascending blow. Put the ball a bit forward in your stance so it's positioned "left of your nose." This means a little off your armpit or left shoulder. With the ball positioned more forward (more toward the instep on your left shoe), the club will come into contact with the ball more on the upswing, producing the ascending blow.

Now focus on your target. In your mind's eye, see precisely where you want the ball to travel. Get a waggle to feel the clubhead. Now line up, staying focused on the target. Standing behind the ball, fix your gaze on the imaginary line running from your ball to the target. Aim the sweet spot of your driver at the target. Your body should be facing the target line.

In this tee shot you'll experience the same considerable lower-body motion of the fairway wood shot. So use this power generator, but as I discussed in chapter 3, be sure not to drive the swing with your hips. I talk to my students about keeping their bodies still by quieting down any erratic motion. The lower body supports, stabilizes, and balances the swing. You also have the maximum wrist hinge and arm swing working for you as your two other power generators. Your distance will come from hinging your wrist correctly and swinging on an inclined plane.

I tell my students to swing smoothly on the tee shot. I encourage them to allow for their own rhythm and to resist the impulse to rush this swing. I suggest that they say to themselves, "Take your time." Keep an even rhythm on your swing no matter what your pace is, fast or slow. Pace is highly idiosyncratic. Mine is fast, while Nancy Lopez has a slower pace to her swing.

When preparing to make the tee shot, I ask a student to think about making her best swing (an example of what sport psychologists call a **performance goal**) rather than trying to make a good shot (an **outcome goal**). I show her how to swing the driver on the

A

B

C

D

E

F

Fig. 26 (A-F). The clubshaft must swing on an inclined plane on the tee shot in particular, in order to hit a straight shot.

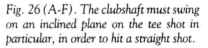

Fig. 27. Tee shot finish position.

inclined plane, as in figure 26, in order to hit the ball straight and solid. The proper finish for the tee shot is shown in figure 27.

The driver is designed with a clubface that is only slightly lofted; this causes the ball to fly in a lower trajectory and then roll. Likewise, because the club-shaft of your driver is longer and the arc of your swing larger, the speed of the club at impact will be greater. For these reasons, the ball will travel farther. In my experience, 155 to 165 yards is a respectable goal for a tee shot, and it is an attainable goal for most women golfers. This distance will help you get to bogey golf quickly as a beginner.

> ON THE FIRST TEE, FOCUS ON YOUR SHOT AND LET GO OF WHAT OTHER PEOPLE ARE THINKING. TAKE YOUR TIME AND GO THROUGH YOUR PRESHOT ROUTINE CAREFULLY.

If you're a more advanced player, you probably already reach 155 yards. Still, I encourage you to practice these shots—to get them consistent and reliable so you lower your scores. Distance off the tee will not necessarily lower your scores. Your goal should be to hit a straight, solid shot.

The preshot routine for a tee shot (or any shot) is important for more advanced players. Remember, a routine is a set of things you do that you don't have to think about consciously; if you have to think about them, then it's not a routine. As I described in chapter 3, this preshot routine consists of actions that let you know you are set; it serves as a GO sign to your brain that says, "I'm ready to hit the golf ball."

After you've refined your established routine, you'll find that you won't feel ready at those times when you've left some things out or rushed through the steps. The message sent to the brain before you swing the club back is "I don't feel ready." And sure enough, if

> AS LONG AS YOU'RE ADVANCING THE BALL AND KEEPING IT IN PLAY, YOU'RE DOING WELL.

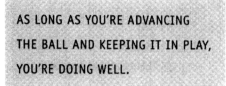

you do bring the club back you'll rush your swing or swing without the clear mental picture you need to hit a shot with confidence.

Let me say a little about the difference between a fairway wood shot and a tee shot, just for your reference. You have a different ball position for each. Of course, with the tee shot, the ball is teed up and easier to hit. At impact you have an ascending blow from your driver. Since the driver is a longer club, it naturally swings farther around you. The fairway wood is shorter than the driver, requiring a steeper or more vertical angle of approach to the ball to get it off the ground.

You won't gain distance by trying to hit the ball harder. That's a swing wrecker. When advanced students come to me for lessons, they often think this way. I remind them that their equipment is what's helping them gain the distance they need. The next part is mastering a smooth, reliable swing that results in solid ball contact. I might say, "You may be struggling with distance because you're using incorrect fundamentals. When you try to hit the ball farther, then, you may just make your mistakes worse."

Especially with beginners, I say, "Don't get hung up on distance. Don't try to hit it far. Work on your accuracy and hitting straight, solid shots. The distance will come later." What you're looking for is consistency, direction, and distance, in that order. This takes time and many repetitions in practice.

It's helpful to know that even the best players in the world all curve the flight of their ball with their full swing. When I played, my natural tendency was to hit the ball

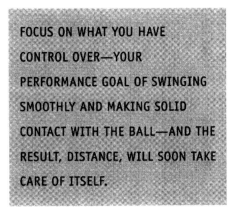

FOCUS ON WHAT YOU HAVE CONTROL OVER—YOUR PERFORMANCE GOAL OF SWINGING SMOOTHLY AND MAKING SOLID CONTACT WITH THE BALL—AND THE RESULT, DISTANCE, WILL SOON TAKE CARE OF ITSELF.

right to left. So when you step up to a tee, always go with your tendencies. If you tend to hit the ball left to right, aim a little left.

Don't fight your tendencies—especially not under pressure, which is when natural inclinations show up in force.

The best swing I ever made in my life came when I was playing with Lou Graham in a team championship in Boca Raton, Florida. We had to birdie the last hole to win the tournament. I was 192 yards from the flag and had to hit a 2-iron for my last shot. Obviously, this is not the shot of choice to win a tournament. I remember saying to myself, "Just take your time and make the best swing you can. Make the very best swing you can." I hit it up there and it landed about 2 feet from the hole; I made the putt for birdie. We tied and won in a sudden-death playoff.

YOU CAN'T CONTROL RESULTS. THIS CAUSES ANXIETY AND CAN WRECK YOUR SWING.

This story is about a time when I was playing professionally. But it illustrates how much better you also can do when you think about the swing itself (a performance goal) and not the outcome. *The outcome can be good or bad, but is likely to be better if you focus on what you can do to make your best possible swing.* You have to be able to say to yourself, "It doesn't matter where this ball goes. I'm going to make a good swing. I'm going to make the best swing I can and let go of the worry about how far the ball goes."

I encourage my students to monitor what they're working on at that moment, not to get distracted by the end results. As Sam discusses in chapter 7, your outcome is likely to be much more to your liking if you focus on what you need to do at each moment and do the best you can. I put it this way: *Grade your swing*

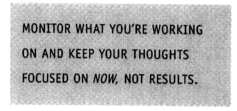

MONITOR WHAT YOU'RE WORKING ON AND KEEP YOUR THOUGHTS FOCUSED ON *NOW*, NOT RESULTS.

and not your shot as you develop your skill. Just monitor what you're working on and keep your thoughts in the present moment.

CHAPTER FIVE

Helpful Additions to Your Three Shots: Putting, Chipping, and Sand Play

The differences between putting and chipping are the club you select and the adjustments you make in your setup. Putts and chips are similar in that there is no lower-body motion or wrist hinge in either one.

1 PUTTING

Putting becomes really important when you see that you are starting to lower your scores. *You lower your scores with the three shots I've been teaching you, especially the pitch shot, which gets you onto the green so you can putt.* When scoring matters, you can start improving your putting and go from, say, 102 to 97, or 95 to 89, by putting more skillfully.

The only way to become skilled at putting is to practice. I recommend spending most of your practice time with putts you should make—the 6-footers and closer. A lot of people will tell you that you need to learn distance putts, and I think that's important, too. I think also it's important to learn how to **lag a putt** (make a long putt with the objective of leaving the ball near the cup). But first you need to learn to hit solid, straight putts and I suggest that you start by focusing your efforts on making 6-footers.

Most people struggle with distance control because they are mis-hitting rather than misreading the putts. It's possible to become a good lag putter by first learning to sink straight 6-foot putts. Distance control then comes with learning how to read the speed of a green and how to make adjustments for the speed of a green, as well as from just playing a *lot* of golf.

I maintain that it will be most useful for you to learn how to swing your putter back and through on a straight path so the putter head hits the ball straight on, rather than delivering a glancing blow that causes sidespin. Gravity, the slope of the lie, and other factors will influence the direction of the ball. Nevertheless, you'll do your best by learning to sink straight 6-foot putts.

To read a green, imagine emptying a bucket of water between you and the hole. Then imagine where the water would go. Would it run to the right? toward you? straight downhill? Whichever way it would run, that's the way your ball is going to go. Now picture whether the water would run fast or trickle. With this exercise you're trying to analyze a green's slope. If the green isn't flat, gravity will have an effect. Locate the sloping area, then try to determine how much slope is present.

Your analysis asks, "Where is my ball in relation to the hole? How is gravity going to influence the way my ball rolls, its speed, and its direction?" Obviously, on a fairly flat green the effect of gravity will be less than on one that slopes a great deal.

You also need to consider how "high" to play your ball. If you dumped imaginary water between you and the hole and it ran very quickly to the right, your ball will of course run very quickly to the right as well. You'll have to play the ball more to the left. That's a general way to aim your putt. You may want to walk halfway to the hole, usually on the low side. From this vantage point, you can observe the length of the putt and see the general slope of the green.

I teach my students both to hit straight putts and to judge the slope of the green so they can analyze the effect of gravity on their putts.

A putt is like a pendulum and uses only one power generator, the arm swing. There is no lower-body motion or wrist hinge. You don't ever want to accelerate the putter because, by definition, a pendulum accelerates to the bottom of its arc at maximum velocity and, naturally, decelerates on the other side of that arc. That's what a pendulum is and that's what a putt is. When you attempt to accelerate the putter, putting becomes a pushing motion, and you'll start shoving your putts to the right. What you do want is a clubhead at maximum velocity at the bottom of its arc; you accomplish this by allowing your putter to move like a pendulum. A pendulum swings in a equidistant path. Your putting stroke should be the same size on the backswing as it is on the forward.

In putting, your grip should be more on the palm than in the fingers. That will eliminate the wrist hinge, which is unnecessary in putting. Your palms face each other with your thumbs on top (see figure 28). Your shoulders face the target line, and the club-face is perpendicular to this line.

You want to position the ball under your left eye because that's the bottom of the arc, the point where the putter head achieves maximum velocity. Your hands are under your sternum. As I said earlier, your only power generator is your arm swing. There is little need to put power on the ball because in putting, the ball is rolling, not flying. You don't need force to get the ball

A

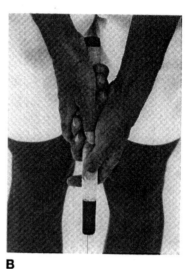

B

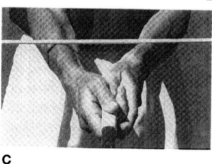

C

Fig. 28. Putting setup. First, the grip—
the putter handle should cross the left
hand, as in (A). The right hand is
placed directly opposite the left, with
the palms facing one another and the
thumbs on top of the grip (B). With
the proper putting grip, you should be
able to balance a stick vertically across
your forearms (C). Set up with your
feet and shoulders square to the target
line (D, E).

D

E

into the air. Your eyes should be located over the ball at the address, and your body should be still.

I recommend that you use my "see and feel" visualization exercise as you prepare to putt. Look at the hole, not the ball, and see where you want the ball to go. I use the phrase *Get it in; or get it close* as my maxim. This exercise with your imagination helps build confidence immediately.

You don't speed up your pace for a putt, but you do need a steady, consistent rhythm. Some golfers think, "One, two, three; back and hit." This little phrase may help you. On the word *back*, start your backstroke. As you say the word *hit*, your putter head should be at impact. The rhythm of your putts will stay the same whether they're long or short. I think the element of rhythm is important—perhaps 40 percent of what you need for accurate putting. The rest? For me it's 10 percent technique and 50 percent confidence, which comes from practice. Fortunately, you can practice indoors at home and save yourself time. I learned to putt by practicing indoors on the carpet on rainy days.

The swing of a putt is a brushing motion with only a very slight descending blow. Putting is an upper-body-oriented stroke in which you take the club straight back from the ball and swing it back through straight at the ball, as in figures 29 and 30. If your putting-swing path is not straight, you'll hit the ball with what's called a glancing blow, causing sidespin and directing the ball away from where you want it to go. You want the distance of the backstroke to equal the distance of the through-stroke, just as a pendulum has an equidistant swinging arc. In good putting, *back equals through*.

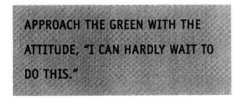
APPROACH THE GREEN WITH THE ATTITUDE, "I CAN HARDLY WAIT TO DO THIS."

Your attitude about putting can make a difference. Approach the green with positive anticipation; believe that you really love to putt. I've found that you really must love to putt to do it well. If you

Fig. 29 *The putting takeaway* . . .

Fig. 30 . . . *ball contact, and follow-through, using arm motion only.*

approach the putt with dread and drooping shoulders, this reluc-
tance will show in your results.

1 CHIPPING

A chip is a putt with a lofted club and a different ball position. When you putt you don't have to get the ball in the air.
When you chip the object is to get the ball slightly off the ground
and into the air. To get the ball airborne, you need a descending
blow. Remember, when the club goes down, the ball goes up.

You use chip shots as stroke savers, just as you do the pitch.
A chip is a shot for moments when you're just off the edge of the
green and would ideally putt, but can't, so you chip instead. In
other words, when you can't putt, you chip. When you can't chip,
you *pitch*. Here's another way to think about the contrast: A putt
rolls on the ground the entire way; a chip rolls on the ground for
most of the way but is in the air for a short time. Remember, any-
time you must get the ball into the air from the grass, you'll need
a descending blow. A chip is a descending blow. You basically
achieve this descending blow with your setup. Figure 31 depicts a
drill I use for helping my students get the feel of the descending
blow in chipping by placing a ball about a foot in front of a piece
of plywood.

The grip for chipping is the overlapping grip shown in chapter 1. You need to play the ball back in your stance, which means
on the "right side of your nose." Play it off your right toe, or off
your right ankle bone. Your hands are always under your sternum,
as in figure 32. If you were to put scales under your feet, 70 percent
of your weight would be on your left side, with 30 percent on your
right. With this weight distribution, your sternum is ahead of the
ball, toward the target. The causes your clubshaft to be at an angle.
The *clubshaft* will be tilted toward the target. You'll feel you can
use your left eye to read the front of the golf ball. This will get *you*
tilted toward the target and help you to achieve the descending

A

B

C

D

Fig. 31. In this chipping drill, I put a piece of wood about a foot behind the ball. To avoid hitting the wood on your chip, you need the correct setup so you can create a descending blow and hit down on the ball. This may feel exaggerated—but it's a very effective drill.

A   **B**

Fig. 32. Set up for the chip with your hands under your sternum, and play the ball off your right outside anklebone.

blow needed to make a correct chip shot. Remember, you are try-ing to swing into the ball in this shot. However, keep in mind the importance of your setup in order to properly execute this shot.

With a chip, you want to send the ball up by striking down on it. Think of it this way: The bottom of your club's arc is always under your sternum—ahead of the ball and "under" the ground. Swinging on this arc, which you create with your setup, creates the descending blow. You want your weight on your left side from the start and throughout this swing.

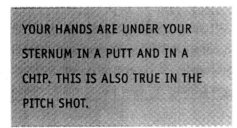
YOUR HANDS ARE UNDER YOUR STERNUM IN A PUTT AND IN A CHIP. THIS IS ALSO TRUE IN THE PITCH SHOT.

Done properly, your setup will position you so that your left eye is looking at the front of the golf ball. Keep your weight in your left hip socket; this will help your arms produce the descending blow. If your shoulders feel more level to the ground, and your weight is distributed equally, your motion will be more sweeping.

You don't have a lot of time in a chip to achieve the descending blow with just your swing *because it's a little swing*. You have to set up for the descending blow before you bring the club back. Keep in mind that it's not a wrist flick. (You're not trying to get the ball up—you're trying to hit the ball down into the ground . . . that's what makes it go up.) Again, a chip has no wrist hinge and no lower-body motion away from or through the ball. It's an arm swing that allows the club to fall to the ball from a short distance off the ground by means of the weight of your arms falling and the clubhead finding the bottom of the arc. Gravity will pull the club to the ball and this gets the ball into the air, where it flies for a short distance. Then it rolls. Thus the motion is still one of trying to "hit the ball into the ground." Refer back to figure 31 for illustrations of the correct motion.

To help new students get the feel of this swing, I teach them a drill that may also be helpful to you. Imagine that a 10-foot laser beam is coming out of the end of your golf club. If your imagination is vivid, you know that you can't let that laser beam hit you when you swing—it would slice right through you. This drill can help you eliminate your wrist flick as well as any scooping action, which is what happens when you inhibit the motion of your lower body but move the golf clubhead with a flicking of your wrist.

For you advanced players, the chip is a stroke saver. Let's say that you've just hit a great shot to the green that's trickled off a bit. You wish you could putt—if you could, you'd get down in 2—but you can't. Because of the **lie,** or the way the grass is, you must chip. (It's always easier to judge the roll of the ball than its flight, by the way. Given this fact, when you can putt, do so. If you can't, then chip.) In order to save par or bogey, chipping is your shot of choice. As you become more proficient at chipping, your scores will get lower.

For you golf-jargon aficionados, the phrase *up and down* refers to chipping: "I'm trying to get up onto the green and down into the hole in 2 shots."

New students ask me what club to use in chipping. My recommendation is to use your favorite medium-lofted club. Here's my theory. With the chip, you have a low-trajectory shot with maximum time on the ground and minimum time in the air. Since it's technically easier to roll the ball than to move it through the air, it's always best to pick a less lofted club and roll the ball. If the flagstick is close to you, however, you can't use a 5- or 7-iron. You may have to use a 9-iron.

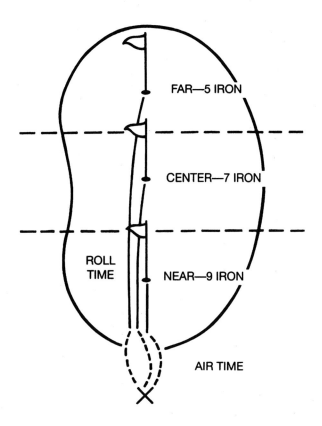

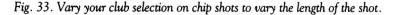

Fig. 33. Vary your club selection on chip shots to vary the length of the shot.

So I endorse the recommendation made by Mike Adam, Instructor at PGA National Golf Club (FL), that if the pin is near, you use a 9-iron. If the pin is far, use a 5-iron. If the pin is in the center of the green, use a 7-iron (see figure 33). If it's a really fast green and you're going downhill, I'd use my pitching wedge with the same setup.

1 SAND PLAY

The sand shot is a full golf swing with a different setup and a club, called a sand wedge, specifically designed to get the ball out of the bunker quickly. This club is fashioned so it can slide or slice through the sand without digging. This is the club you'll use when you find yourself in a sandy predicament. Your goal for your shot is first to get out, or second to hit the ball nearly out of the bunker, in that order. If you send your ball out every time you use your sand wedge, you'll certainly lower your scores.

You'll need a firm foundation as you make this full swing, and you want to be positioned with your feet lower than the ball, so that you hit the sand rather than the ball. Your setup (shown in figure 34) accomplishes this when you follow these steps:

1. Lower yourself into the sand by scrunching your feet down into it about 2 inches.

2. Use the overlapping grip taught in chapter 1.

3. Open your clubface. Dial the club handle to the right until you see the score lines on the face of the club point toward your left toe.

4. Aim your toe line to the left of the target.

5. Play the ball off your left toe (that is, your ball position is off your left toe).

6. Take a full swing, making sure that you swing along the toe line (as in figure 35).

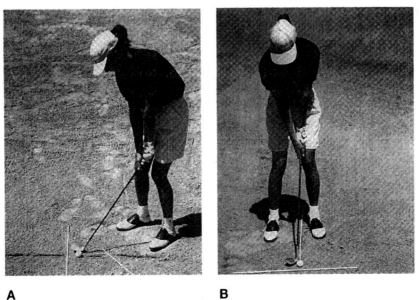

A   B

Fig. 34. Sand setup. Open your stance, dial the clubface to the right so the score lines point toward your left toe, and play the ball off your left toe. In this sequence, I have deliberately kept my feet on the top of the sand so you can see their position—but for stability, scrunch your own feet down a couple of inches into the sand.

Fig. 35. Swing along the toe line.

The number one rule of sand play that there is no ball contact. You are displacing sand rather than hitting the ball directly. Your sand wedge is designed specifically to slide or skid through the sand and take the ball out of the bunker with it (as shown in figure 36). Because of your setup position your feet are below the ball, so you don't need to worry about aiming or hitting behind the ball, taking sand, or trying to hit behind the ball. If you lower yourself in the sand, you will automatically take sand. Your setup position and your equipment will help you do that. The novelty of sand play makes it important that you spend some time with your instructor getting this shot right.

Try this drill for sand play: Make circles in the sand. Swing and try to hit the sand from within the circle onto the green. Once you accomplish this, put a ball in the center of the circle and once again, try to hit or take the sand onto the green. The ball will be carried along for the ride.

The goals of sand play are to get out, get on, and get close, in that order. You want to get out of the sand, onto the green, and close to the flagstick as expediently as possible. Remember you are not hitting the ball—you are displacing sand. And oh yes, be sure to rake the bunker after you've hit your shot.

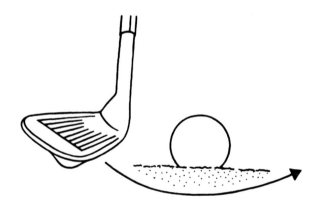

Fig. 36 *The sand wedge follows a path under the ball—there is no ball contact on a sand shot.*

CHAPTER SIX

A Woman's Guide to Saving Time

I don't believe in long practice sessions. They bore a lot of people and they rarely fit into a woman's busy schedule. So please don't try two hours of practicing. I don't find that length of time practicing alone to be beneficial for my students—unless, of course, they're extremely good players with lots of time. If you truly want to make some improvements in your swing or learn something new quickly, go to golf school for a long weekend. Two-day or weeklong golf schools are great ways for beginners to become quick studies. These schools create the opportunity for intensive learning with lots of instruction.

Use a full-length mirror indoors to check your posture and setup. I use a portable mirror a lot in my lessons, one about 6 feet high, to help my students check visually on how they're doing.

Use your time in front of the television to practice your grip. In fact, there are several things you can practice indoors. My instructor, Fred, had me practice my full swing at home a hundred times each day, with the instruction, "Back and through, back and through." And on the tour, we found ways to remain focused on our game when the course was closed after dark or for rainy weather. I remember us putting down the hallways of our hotels. I recall Merle Breer telling me how she learned to hit a high, soft wedge shot. She showed me that she'd practiced hitting this particular wedge shot off the hard carpet onto the bed in her hotel room. She asked me to try. At first I said, "No way. I'll top it and break a window." But I did finally try her unique method and to this day, that's how I picture this wedge shot. It's actually how I learned to hit a little flop shot. You may not want to practice at this intensity level, of course, because your goals now are different from what mine were then. But you will find it helpful to practice your swing at home for a few minutes a day once your instructor has you pretty comfortable with it.

Rainy days are a great time to practice putting indoors on the carpet. Fred had me do this, too, on our carpet at home, which was a good approximation of a putting surface.

An important factor in saving your time generally is to let go of the myths you may have heard from others, however well meaning, about how you should play golf. The Three-Shot Golf system was created to save you time and keep you in the game by getting down to only the things that work and work reliably for women. You will find it helpful to deprogram such theories (heard in past lessons or read in golf books) as these:

- Keep your head down. *This can certainly wreck your swing. With your head too far down, you feel like you can't rotate your body.*

- Delay the club. *This won't work, because you're trying to create momentum and speed on a full swing.*

- Keep your left arm straight. *True, if you remember that your arm is extended throughout most of the swing. However, on the forward swing, your left arm "folds." The notion of straightness generates muscle tension for a lot of women.*
- Use your legs. *Your legs are, in fact, just supporting and stabilizing your swing.* I have demonstrated to classes that I can hit the ball while sitting in a chair almost as far as I can hit the ball while on my feet.
- Drive the ball with your hips. *You don't hit the ball with your hips. You hit the ball with your club.* Don't allow your body to get too far ahead of your arm swing.

These theories are not very useful to you, and trying to implement them is likely to waste your time. Sort out the confusion with your instructor and stick to the shots that really work to get you to bogey golf or better, quickly—so you'll stay in the game.

I think it's better to have a thirty- to forty-minute practice session three times per week. Commit yourself to the time that you actually have. Realize that the only way you develop a new habit or skill is through repetition. I suggest that you focus on pitch shots. Get busy on your fairway wood shots right away. Work on your 6-foot putts. I wouldn't put time into anything else. Forget practicing shots you only rarely use. Eliminate the 4-, 3-, and 2-iron shots and your 3-wood fairway shots. This will save you time right away.

You might use your time in this manner. Begin by warming up with your pitch shots. Then take a few shots with your irons; proceed on to a substantial number of fairway wood shots off the tees and, when you feel comfortable, take these shots off the grass. Hit fifteen tee shots with the club you usually use for these shots— your driver, your 3-wood, or even your 5-wood. To end your session, practice your 6-foot putts for ten minutes.

Make each practice count. Include your preshot routine in your practice shots. Build up your confidence by working on

things with your favorite clubs. Always concentrate on the performance goal of making good swings; let go of your concern with
outcomes. Focus on finding clubs you like and are becoming successful with; these are the ones you'll use when you play. At the
driving range, work on "virtual shots" from the course. If you're a
good visualizer, picture the course and where you want the ball to
go. Then fly it there.

You might consider having a friend or your instructor video-
tape your practice sessions or lessons so that you can make corrections and enjoy your signs of improvement. Make it a habit to
debrief each round with a trusted friend or your instructor. Limit the
time you allow yourself to be upset about a round that was a disappointment. Look for fixes and work on them, but don't overdo the
analysis. You might keep a logbook of corrections and suggestions
from your instructor and notes after your own practice sessions.

Inch your way into keeping score. When you're starting out,
you don't have to mark a scorecard. Remember, there's no rule
that says you must keep score. Likewise, inch your way into tournament and match play. If you can, go first and think about playing one shot at a time.

To maximize your practice time, monitor what you're working
on. Set up a "swing practice station" at the driving range. Use an
aiming aid to attain the correct alignment. First, lay a clubshaft down
on the ground, parallel to the target line. Aim the clubface perpendicular to the target line. Now align your body to the clubface. See if
you're ready. If so, swing. Have a target for each shot so you can monitor the direction and shape of the shot you're practicing.

On days you're hitting the ball badly on full swings, stop and
go back to your pitch shot, or stop and go back to your favorite golf
club and practice with that. Sit down and take a break. Go into
the clubhouse and have a little rest. This is not the time to try to
hit the ball harder. I don't want you practicing failure. Try to end
each practice session on a positive note so you'll stay encouraged
rather than becoming discouraged.

If you're really having trouble with something, schedule a lesson with your instructor and enlist his or her help in sorting out the problem. It's also a great idea to practice with your instructor alongside; go together sometimes to the driving range.

> REMEMBER THAT NOT EVERY PRACTICE SESSION WILL FEEL SUCCESSFUL. THAT'S TRUE FOR ANY ATHLETE. LET YOURSELF SHAKE OFF A DISAPPOINTING PRACTICE, KNOWING THERE IS ANOTHER ONE.

I have found that it's important to establish a certain kind of learning environment for my women students—one in which they aren't judged for making mistakes. Rather, I encourage women to feel that they can risk swinging hard and perhaps making a mistake. I want my students to experience success early on with the miniature swing, then move on to the full swing. If they struggle with the full swing, we go back to the small swing and reestablish success there before moving on. You should do the same.

I remember teaching a Mrs. Thompson, who was eighty years old when I gave her lessons. She actually had quite a good golf swing and must have played a very respectable game when she was younger. She did need help with her clubhead speed, which was only about 20 miles per hour.

I told Mrs. Thompson that in order to increase her clubhead speed she needed to do two things: move her body more and hit the ball harder. She said, "Yes, dear." But hitting the ball hard, or hitting anything hard, was a foreign concept to her. So I suggested that she try to make some sound at impact. I got her some empty milk cartons and asked her to swing at them.

She hit milk cartons for a while and began to feel comfortable hitting them harder and harder. She seemed to develop a sense of reckless abandon hitting this kind of target, and her clubhead speed got considerably faster. I switched her back to hitting balls and the good feeling of hitting a target hard carried over. She went after swings a little harder, and was less worried than before about mis-hitting the ball—so she hit it harder. Then we worked on her hitting it straighter. She added about 20 yards to her drive, which made her very happy.

Make sure that you have scheduled your practice times when you aren't too tired, mentally or physically. Golf is a demanding game, and you want to bring some good energy with you when you come to work on your shots. I do remind students that this is play and not meant to be a job, however. I want their lessons and playing time to be enjoyable.

Some women have expectations for their golf games that might be more appropriate for their careers. Remember that this is your recreation, not your career. Reconfigure your expectations accordingly.

When a student asks me how long it will take her to learn to play the game, I ask, "How many hours do you have to put into it?" I want my students manage their expectations about playing well but also to understand the implication of my question. They can get good more quickly if they can put in lots of hours. Developing the habits that lead to great golf requires repetition.

Speaking of frustration, I learned from Fred Wetmore, the professional who taught me the game, a very important principle that helped me as I was mastering my game. Without telling me exactly why he was doing so, when he saw that I was getting upset with my technique, he would instruct me to switch to practicing something else. You should do the same. When you get frustrated in a practice session, switch to a task you're likely to experience more success in. Then come back to the skill that was frustrating you.

> WHEN YOU FEEL FRUSTRATED AFTER ATTEMPTING A SKILL, WORK ON SOMETHING ELSE. COME BACK TO THAT SKILL LATER.

For a busy person who has realistic expectations, what are some other ways to save time? Consider playing just nine holes in the late afternoon with friends at your playing level. At that time of the day and with gals playing much like you do, there's less pressure. Also, consider "giving putts" to speed up play rather than taking the time to putt out. Offer other "gimmies" when it makes sense to do so. If you're having trouble, go to the 100-yard marker and play from there. Remember, *nowhere in the rules of golf is a statement that you must keep score.* Not doing so will save time as well as taking the pressure off.

If you have the opportunity to play with someone who's a better golfer than you, be sure that you inform this person of your level, especially if you're a beginner. If you're more experienced but still feel you have a lot to learn, explain this as well. You don't need to go into the gory details, but do accurately inform your prospective partner. If this person is someone who can be patient, by all means partner up. You might even consider playing with your instructor, paying him or her the hourly fee for the time. This is an excellent way to learn to transfer skills from the driving range to the golf course. You'll quickly see that golf consists of much more than just swinging clubs. Your pro can help you learn course strategy while you're there.

You can also save time by practicing on a par-3 course or one of those little executive courses. These are great places to get better. You don't have to play eighteen holes on a championship golf course every time. As a beginner it might be better for you to hit lots of golf balls before you go out to the course.

REMEMBER, THERE'S NO DEFENSE ON THE DRIVING RANGE, SO IT'S A GOOD PLACE TO GET YOUR CONFIDENCE UP. AT A GOLF COURSE YOU'LL HAVE OTHER PLAYERS, HAZARDS, AND LOTS OF OTHER DISTRACTIONS TO DEAL WITH.

If you get into trouble during a game, set your mind to making one shot, a recovery shot, to get back into play. Don't spend too much time fretting over the hazard or the mess you're in. Don't attempt heroics and then take an 8 on the hole. Keep your head, remind yourself to be patient, and focus on what to *do*. Let your goal be getting back into play quickly and then moving along, leaving the mistake behind you.

It also helps you save time if you play to your strengths when you're in doubt. If you love your 5-wood, use that. Pick your favorite club to advance the ball. If you can't get it to the green or to a safe landing area, don't go for it. Play short or lay back. Always play for bogey; it will never hurt you to do so. You can even allow yourself to go for double bogey. Just stay away from making an 8; it's an attitude wrecker.

If you're, say, 150 yards out, and you're not confident that you can fly the ball that far, take out your 7-wood and play short. Then take your favorite pitch shot and put the ball on the green. Don't waste time trying to hit a shot you've never hit before. Play for bogey.

Remember that *people* on the course, not just men, get frustrated with golfers who are playing too slowly. Keep up a good pace. Be ready to hit your shot when it's your turn, while still having fun. You can do your serious socializing with friends later, either when you're in the golf cart or back at the clubhouse.

Don't just sit in the golf cart until it's your turn. It's your responsibility to be ready to hit when it's your turn. It's a good idea to pull your golf cart up to the back of the green. Get your club out of your bag, walk smartly, and get into position. Be ready. After the hole is finished and all the players are "in the hole," quickly make your way to the next hole.

It's also your responsibility to keep up with the group ahead of you, and I recommend you focus on this rather than worrying about what's happening behind you. If you're keeping up with the group ahead but the group behind is pushing you, don't get concerned. Of course, sometimes it makes sense for the group in back of you to play through. Allow that graciously.

Plan your next shot, but don't waste time analyzing it or complaining about it. Just get ready to do your preshot routine and swing. Know your score and keep track of how others in your group are doing. As long you're keeping the ball in play, you're doing well. Enjoy yourself and keep moving.

Keep in mind the purpose of practice: It isn't for reaching perfection, it's for the expansion of your skills and the development of your confidence. Give yourself a chance when you're learning something new. Remember that repetition is the *only* way to develop your skills. Please keep in mind that not every day on the course will be a wonderful experience. Some days you just won't have it. This happens to all golfers. It's part of mastering a sport and certainly a part of the process of learning.

Winter can be a great time to take lessons and hit a lot of balls if you live in a part of the country where this is possible. Or go to an indoor driving range; you'll find these in some cities back East. Summer is a time for playing; if you can, use the winter months for working on skills and developing the habits you'll need to enjoy your playing.

> MY TEACHER, FRED WETMORE, USED TO TELL ME TO WORK FOR PROGRESS, NOT PERFECTION. HE'D SAY, "IT DOESN'T COME EASY. KEEP WORKING AT IT. YOU'LL GET IT BUT NOT NECESSARILY WHEN YOU EXPECT TO."

I want to share a story about woman who came to me for lessons. She was the president of a company, dealt in high finance, and was very successful. She had never played sports as a kid and hadn't attempted anything as an adult before this time. Beginning a challenging sport at this point in her life was her "last frontier." I had enormous respect for her courage in taking this on after such an outstanding career history.

She appreciated my support for her persistence in coming

back for lessons with what little time she had. She had time for one bucket of balls after a lesson. But she kept coming back.

I also think of a woman back East who asked me for lessons, saying she had never played before. Her goal for the summer was to "play nine holes." So we started in with her taking three lessons a week. It was tough and we had some ups and downs. But she hung in there. She kept coming back. We kept addressing her weak areas. She learned the short shots. She learned the long shots. And finally, we got her out on the course to play one hole. Then we played three holes. Sure enough, by the end of the summer we played nine holes.

I share these stories with you as a way of encouraging you to find a pro who will support you and will go out on the golf course with you. Your pro can help you with the 75 percent of the game unrelated to your golf swing, like course management. Your pro can help you find game-improving equipment and assist you in remaining persistent during your inevitable ups and downs.

CHAPTER SEVEN

Mental Strategies for Women

USEFUL ON THE GOLF COURSE AND ELSEWHERE IN LIFE

CHAPTER BY
SANDRA FOSTER, PH.D.

A glance at the golf books displayed in the sports section of any large bookstore will reveal many on instruction and quite a few on the mental game of golf. Two authors in particular could be helpful to improving the mental side of your game: Dr. Bob Rotella and his collection of stories of golfing greats told in *Golf Is a Game of Confidence*, and Fred Shoemaker's advice in *Extraordinary Golf*. Or to appreciate the mystical nature of the game, read Michael Murphy's *Golf in the Kingdom* and his tale of Shivas Irons and the Zen way of approaching golf.

This chapter tells you how to apply several performance-enhancement techniques to your game, and how to integrate optimistic thinking into your learning process as well as on the course. I share these ideas with you from the perspective of someone who came to golf later in life and who had the opportunity, as a beginner, to put into practice the sports-psychology techniques that were already familiar to me. I think both beginners and advanced players will find these strategies helpful; they can enhance the mental side of any sport and even make a difference in your work life.

1 DEVELOPING PERSISTENCE AS YOU LEARN TO PLAY GOLF

Golf is such a complex game that you will need skills in persistence to stay involved in it. What will help you develop the staying power that is called persistence? A personal desire to do something, a commitment to both learning and implementing the lessons, support for your doing it (internal and external), and skill at getting back on your feet when things get challenging. Let me take you through each step as it applies to your golf game. Keep in mind that these steps can be applied to other aspects of your life: your career; your hobbies; any pursuit that takes you out of your comfort zone, such as giving speeches or writing for an audience; or navigating your way through a challenging life event, like taking care of a loved one who's ill.

Ask yourself the following questions as you think about each of these steps. You may find it helpful to write down your answers.

1. What are my reasons for playing golf?

   Are these reasons my own? Or am I playing golf for someone else?

   Am I gaining personal satisfaction from learning and playing, or is someone else's concern with my game the reason I work at it?

Of course, many of us take up the game because of someone else's interest in it, and we want to maintain that person's interest in us. Many players, including Janet herself, had parents who played and encouraged them to start. In some other situations, it's a boyfriend, husband, partner, friend, or business associate who already plays and suggests that we join in. Having another person to get you initiated is a great way to begin learning the game. To persist in the process of skill development, however, you need your own personal reasons for showing up, again and again, at the driving range and the course.

How can you make golf your own game if you answered the questions and found you are playing with someone else's needs in mind?

Think about what benefits of the sport are real for you already, or could be. Consider whether golf can become your passion and, therefore, a shared interest between you and the person who got you started. Can golf be a business tool for you, if you play in tournaments with coworkers or rounds with customers? Can golf be a source of new friendships? Can golf serve as an individual challenge to you, something you choose in order to enhance your athletic skills and personal development?

> SITUATION: I'M NOT ABLE TO DUPLICATE THE SHOT THAT MY INSTRUCTOR IS DEMONSTRATING. I CAN SAY TO MYSELF, "OKAY, THIS IS TOUGH—AND I *WILL* GET IT EVENTUALLY. STAY OPTIMISTIC."

Do what you can to find your own reasons for playing golf and your own source of gratification from the game. That way, when things get tough and you "lose it"—as Janet spoke about earlier—you can persist by reminding yourself that it is you whom you do this for, and it is you who can feel proud when you overcome a difficulty.

2. Have I made a commitment to the time, effort, expense, and difficult tasks necessary to develop my game?

Recall what Janet suggested in chapter 1: that you consider devoting twelve weeks to advancing your game, or the equivalent of one summer. This period of time could include attending a golf school to launch your efforts, or signing up for an intensive series of lessons and clinics. Alternatively, you could extend your timeline over many more months, committing yourself to one lesson or more per week plus regular practice sessions and a weekly round.

SITUATION: I HAD A PRETTY GOOD FULL SWING AND NOW I'M SWINGING WILDLY ALL OVER THE PLACE. I CAN SAY TO MYSELF, "EVEN THE PROS LOSE IT ON OCCASION. STAY WITH IT." I CAN RECOGNIZE MY FRUSTRATION, TRY TO SHAKE IT OFF, AND KEEP MY PERSPECTIVE. I CAN WORK ON SOMETHING ELSE, LIKE MY PITCH SHOT, AND COME BACK TO THE FULL SWING A LITTLE LATER.

The point here is to make a commitment to getting serious about learning and playing the game. This agreement with yourself helps set the stage for taking up such a challenging game as golf.

Sign up for golf school dates or clinics, and send in your deposit. Or locate an instructor and make a schedule of lesson dates. For most of us, commitment requires that we make golf a priority activity. This isn't easily done if you have a career and family. Think of creative ways to carve out the time you'll need to acquire your skills. Refer back to chapter 6, on saving time, for ideas that might make it possible to commit to playing golf.

3. Even when I have my own reasons for playing, who can be my supporters as I pursue the game of golf?

   Can I create my own internal source of support, a kind of inner coach to help me persist in my game?

Psychologists have observed the benefits of what they call "social support" for people who are ill or injured, and the importance of a "people network" to anyone's well-being. When we have one or more people around who care about us and cheer us on, we do much better.

Who can be your backer as you take on the challenges of golf? Do you already know other women golfers at your level with whom you can play and attend golf school and clinics? Can you join a women's league whose members have levels of skill and interests similar to yours? Can you join a group of women golfers in your area who get together mainly to socialize, if that's a better fit for you? Do you have a woman acquaintance or friend who is pursuing another sport, but with whom you can share stories and encouragement?

It's easier to persist in golf when you have a buddy to help you regain perspective when you've lost yours. Having someone to celebrate your successes with adds to your enjoyment of the game. And being caught up in the process of learning with a companion at your level can give each of you a valuable sounding board.

Can you imagine the benefits of deliberately coaching yourself from the inside out? Winning athletes know how much this helps. You too can develop your own internal mentor who could encourage you with statements such as, "Remember your commitment to yourself to do this."

1 DEVELOPING OPTIMISM AS A GOLFER (A PRETTY GOOD IDEA FOR OTHER AREAS OF LIFE, TOO)

A crucial element of staying persistent in learning the skills of golf is your internal language. This is especially important when you need to come back after a disappointing lesson or round.

Let me turn to some questions that will help you figure out what mentally contributes to the great moments in your game— and the awful ones.

A. *When I have trouble in a lesson and can't perform the skill, do I think this situation is temporary?* Or am I convinced that I'm stuck in this bad situation for many days or weeks?

B. *When I leave the driving range after a morning practice session that feels like a flop, do I think of that event as an upsetting part of my day, but believe my hours at work and at home will still be okay?* Or do I predict that the rest of the day will be a bust because I couldn't the hit ball well?

C. After finishing a round that was a real disappointment, do I torment myself with blame and ridicule for playing so badly, even saying to myself that I should give up the game altogether? *Or do I consider factors in the round that can be fixed, and possibly some external circumstances (wind, noisy players behind my foursome) that may have contributed to my less-than-hoped-for performance?*

D. When my instructor tells me I just had a great lesson, do I think, "Oh, that's just today. It won't happen again tomorrow"? *Or do I believe that other good lessons will follow?*

E. When I leave the driving range after a particularly outstanding morning practice, do I drive away thinking, "Oh, that was nice, but now it's off to an impossible meeting or messy situation with my family/partner/husband"? *Or do I think, "That was excellent! The rest of my day looks pretty good, too," and predict that a number of things will go well?*

F. After a very successful round, do I shrug off the compliments of my friends by saying, "I just got lucky today. You really inspire me, that's all," and let any personal credit for the positive outcome fade away? *Or do I listen to their complimentary feedback and respond with, "Thanks. I've been working on my swing and it has been getting better"?*

These questions can give you a sense of your explanatory style related to your golf game—and perhaps, to other parts of your life as well. *Explanatory style* is the term coined by University of Pennsylvania psychologist Dr. Martin Seligman, whose cutting-edge research looked at the effect of a person's explanations for events, both good and bad. Explanatory style, Dr. Seligman wrote in his books *Learned Optimism* and *The Optimistic Child*, could be either pessimistic or optimistic. I think you'll find both books fascinating and recommend the second one to you to learn more about what I'm discussing here.

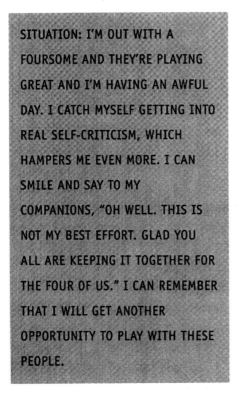

SITUATION: I'M OUT WITH A FOURSOME AND THEY'RE PLAYING GREAT AND I'M HAVING AN AWFUL DAY. I CATCH MYSELF GETTING INTO REAL SELF-CRITICISM, WHICH HAMPERS ME EVEN MORE. I CAN SMILE AND SAY TO MY COMPANIONS, "OH WELL. THIS IS NOT MY BEST EFFORT. GLAD YOU ALL ARE KEEPING IT TOGETHER FOR THE FOUR OF US." I CAN REMEMBER THAT I WILL GET ANOTHER OPPORTUNITY TO PLAY WITH THESE PEOPLE.

In the six questions above, I've given the optimistic explanation in italics. Check your answers to see how many pessimistic and optimistic answers fit for you in this very informal assessment.

Explanatory style for both good and bad events has three dimensions: *time*, or how long the event lasts; *pervasiveness*, or the extent to which the event generalizes or "spreads" to other events; and *personalization*, or seeing yourself as the cause of the event, rather than seeing that other people and external circumstances play a role in making something happen.

Questions A and D deal with the dimension of time. Someone with a pessimistic explanatory style explains a bad situation as one that will last a long time, even permanently. This leads to the person feeling upset and hopeless. Those with a more optimistic explanatory style, on the other hand, explain the unpleasant outcome as temporary and predict that tomorrow will be a better day.

Questions B and E concern the dimension of pervasiveness, or how much of life is affected by one event. The person with a more pessimistic explanatory style thinks that one bad event will affect other parts of life in a negative way. Think of the analogy of dropping a bit of ink (one bad event) into a glass of water; the ink darkens all of it (everything now looks bad).

A pessimistic explanation of a frustrating practice session quickly spreads to a prediction of a tough day at work and lots of hassles at home that evening. If a pessimistic outlook really starts to snowball, the person may begin thinking that just about everything in life is bad. Hopelessness and giving up—on golf, and possibly on other activities—may result.

In contrast, people with a more optimistic explanatory style limit a negative explanation to just that one unpleasant practice session. They try to think about the good things going on in their lives, and figure that they can still have a good day elsewhere. Optimists might also perform what sports psychologists call a "success review," recalling more satisfying practices and great rounds, or taking an inventory of recent wins on the course and in other parts of life to get perspective on the negative event.

The personalization dimension is being asked about in questions C and F. A person with a pessimistic explanatory style will walk away from a bad round thinking, "I'm terrible at this!" or "I don't have what it takes to play golf," and get stuck in excessive self-blame. Other factors that may have contributed to the poor round are ignored resulting in no attempt to remedy the technical problems.

SITUATION: I HAVE AN UNUSUALLY GREAT LESSON. I CAN THANK MY INSTRUCTOR AND THINK TO MYSELF "I'M LOOKING FORWARD TO MORE DAYS LIKE THIS"—DAYS THAT KEEP MY SPIRITS UP IN THE UNEVEN PROCESS OF LEARNING GOLF.

Now, before you get the idea that I'm telling you to blame everyone else for your bad round, let me set things straight. This is not about avoiding personal responsibility; it's about being aware that constant self-blame can lead to giving up.

Practicing optimism means taking responsibility for your part in events, and looking for things that you can fix and make better. But it also means looking at the influence of outside circumstances and other people in a situation. This approach leads to better problem solving and greater persistence.

Research shows us that highly personalized self-blame in the form of beliefs like "I'm a loser" or "I'm just worthless" puts a damper on self-improvement. Instead, the self-blame leads to self-doubt and abandoning challenging activities like golf.

Golfers practicing optimism look at their faults in order to find fixes and improve. They also think about what happened and what made the round difficult. By considering external circumstances, optimists aren't making excuses for a poor round. Next time, they will factor external influences—such as wind speed, the lie, and course difficulty—into their playing.

What does this have to do with you and your golf scores? A lot.

Your explanatory style has a significant impact on your enjoyment of golf and your persistence in developing your skills. Likewise, your explanatory style affects your view of your career and your personal relationships—even your health.

The connection between an optimistic explanatory style and athletic success was demonstrated in a recent study of nationally ranked collegiate swimmers. Dr. Seligman began by administering to young men and women the test he'd developed to measure explanatory style. Then the swimmers were asked to swim their best event, while their coaches were told to give them "false feedback" about how they'd performed. The coaches did so, telling the athletes that they'd raced more slowly than was actually the case. The swimmers had a rest and then were told to swim their event again.

On this second try, the swimmers who'd tested as optimists swam the same or faster times than they had on their first attempt. Their optimistic style allowed them to shake off the negative outcome. In fact, they came back stronger! In stark contrast, the swimmers who'd scored as pessimists swam more slowly on the second try. The false feedback appeared to discourage them and they seemed to give up.

How does this research study relate to you? If your explanation for a poor round or a disappointing practice is optimistic, you'll make a stronger comeback. You'll persist. You'll believe that the negative outcome is temporary, limited to that just that one golf outing and not the rest of your life. (In psychology lingo, the pervasiveness of the bad event is perceived as narrow or limited in its scope.) As a golfer practicing optimism, you'll look at what you did that didn't work so you can make needed changes. You'll also consider the influence of other people and external circumstances in deciding on a different approach.

When you play a good round or come away from a great lesson, an optimistic explanatory style can also help. Say to yourself that these positive outcomes will last; they are enduring. Also, think of yourself as someone who has enduring good qualities and a talent for golf and other things. Allow the pervasiveness of your positive events to spread. Don't see these happy moments in golf as the only positive things happening in your life; think of your life as positive in a more global way.

SITUATION: I'VE BEEN REALLY WHACKING BALLS SOLIDLY AT THE DRIVING RANGE AND EVEN NOTICE AN ADMIRING GLANCE OR TWO IN MY DIRECTION. I CAN TELL MYSELF THAT I AM IMPROVING. I CAN RECALL THIS PLEASANT DAY AT A LATER TIME WHEN THE GOING IS A LITTLE TOUGHER.

Practicing optimism in the personalizing dimension means taking credit for your good outcomes, accepting compliments, and not letting yourself pass off your happy results as mere luck.

How can this optimistic explanatory style affect your life outside golf?

In a study of sales executives in a large midwestern company, the most optimistic among them sold up to 84 percent more than their pessimistic counterparts. The optimists also stayed with the company longer.

So developing optimism has implications for your work life—and your health. In another study, college students who tested as optimists were shown to have fewer communicable illnesses, such as colds and flu, than their pessimistic classmates. But the really good news was that when the pessimistic students were taught the skills of an optimistic explanatory style, their health improved. They got sick less often, like the optimists.

That's the best part: Optimism is a learned skill. You can learn the fundamentals of optimism for yourself. You'll improve your mental approach to learning and playing golf, see greater success in other areas of your life as well—and maybe even catch fewer colds!

Your explanatory style developed from what you observed and took in during early experiences within your family and at school. You may have learned a pessimistic explanatory style because of hardships or early losses in childhood. However, *you can work at learning optimism at any point in life, even right now.* Practicing optimism can enhance the quality of your life and help your golf game!

So how to start? Review your answers to questions 4A through 4F. If you find you have more of an optimistic view, that's great. Keep it going. If you find your responses to be more pessimistic, take heart that a new way of thinking can be learned. Consider reading *The Optimistic Child* to learn the steps of developing optimism—right now. In the short term, and related to your golf, study the sidebars in this chapter for ideas about keeping yourself on the optimistic track.

1 DEVELOPING YOUR ABILITY TO FOCUS AND CONCENTRATE

Psychologist Mark Frazier recently reviewed 175 references on golf psychology. He concluded that the ability to focus was one of the most important factors in playing great golf.

Let me give you three definitions used frequently in psychology:

To focus: To take notice of one thing in particular by narrowing your attention to just that thing and managing any distractions that might interfere.

A distraction: Something that diverts your attention away from the object of your desired focus, such as your golf shot.

To concentrate: To sustain your focus for a specified period of time.

Golf-psychology experts such as Bob Rotella have talked about the importance of focusing on one swing at a time and staying in the present moment as you do so. Having "present-moment awareness" means that you take your attention away from what has already occurred—like your last shot, which upset you—and also that you keep yourself from thinking too far into the future, like worrying about your final score. Instead, you focus your awareness on what is happening *right now*.

> THINK ABOUT YOUR EXTERNAL CIRCUMSTANCES. CHANGE THOSE THAT ARE CHANGEABLE AND COME TO TERMS WITH THOSE THAT AREN'T.

This focus on the present gives you your best chance to perform well, because your mind is tuned in and your body isn't reliving those awful minutes in the sand (that happened three holes back or even three months back).

I approach focus from the point of view of managing distractions as a tactic for keeping yourself in the here and now. Distractions can be thought of as external or internal. External distractions are things outside yourself—noise, wind, air temperature, other people's performances. Internal distractions are inner experiences such as thoughts, emotions, and the physical sensations that accompany them; a less-than-optimal state of physical well-being; and excessive concern with the approval of other people.

In my work with athletes and others who must deliver high-level performances, I find that people focus more easily when they know *why* they are performing. If you apply this to yourself, you'll see that you're likely focus more effectively if you're clear about your reasons for playing golf—reasons that are personal and important to you. (This also helps you persist, as I mentioned earlier.)

Let me give you some quick pointers for managing internal distractions.

One way you can manage physical sensations is by regulating your breath, even if asthma or other respiratory problems make this challenging. Learning to slow your breathing so that you neither hold your breath nor hyperventilate is a valuable tool in managing emotions like anger and fear.

You can practice by counting your breaths per minute using the second hand of a watch or clock. Slowing to 10 to 12 breaths per minute may help you feel calmer. Slowing your breath even further, to 8 or 9 per minute, may make you feel even more relaxed.

A second way to manage internal distractions is the cognitive or self-talk approach. Simply substitute helpful internal coaching statements for the critical self-talk that disrupts your focus. Here are two of my favorite self-statements from my friend and colleague Gary Mack, who consults with major-league baseball teams and the Phoenix Fire Department:

YOU MUST BE PRESENT TO WIN.
BREATHE AND FOCUS.

When things get rough or you are in the rough, I encourage you to talk to yourself like a caring internal coach. **Use phrases that feel helpful to you as you regulate your breathing.**

You can also increase your overall physical balance and well-being by getting sufficient sleep, eating nutritious food, avoiding excess caffeine (which can make you feel jittery and cold), and coming to the course or your lesson when you felt physically well.

If you're choking—experiencing a dramatic decrease in your customary performance level—you may be able to pull yourself out of it by telling yourself, "Get into the game and out of comparisons." Measuring your progress by someone else's standards is a source of misery. Make *you* your basis of comparison. How well are you doing compared with last week or last year?

On the other hand, objective comparisons—done before you walk onto the course or driving range—may help you understand what a certain golfer does to execute a particular great shot. You can then assess how your own performance compares to this objective standard. Subjective comparisons—"She's better than I am, she's more attractive," and so on—pull you off focus and can impair your ability to deliver what you do know how to do.

How is it possible to ignore external distractions such as the voices of other golfers, bright sunlight, or heat? First, dress according to the weather, with adequate rain gear if you need it. Shield yourself from the heat with hats or visors and sunscreen. Talk to yourself convincingly about the importance of your own view of your game versus someone else's view so that an external distraction like a snide remark doesn't become an internal distraction eating away at your insides. (You can speak to this person later if you feel it might be advisable.)

Focus on where you want the ball to go, as Janet has suggested. Tell yourself, "Stay in the game," if you hear comments around you. Try Gary's statement—"Breathe and focus." Keep yourself in the present moment with phrases like, "Just this shot. This one. This one, right now."

Develop your preshot routine to make it so automatic that you can just flow through it, getting yourself into the "zone" or "flow" as sports psychologists call this wonderful state. Focus on the waggle, the physical feeling of your club in your hands, to pull you out of negative thoughts. Getting "physical and wordless" with your actions can help as you prepare to make your shot.

Finally, managing distractions, both internal and external, is aided by keeping things in perspective. It even helps the masters when they do so. Remember, "This is only a game. It is not a matter of life or death. My reputation isn't riding on this round." Beyond this, remember that having fun is one of the reasons you took up this game in the first place.

JANET'S BEST TAKES ON RULES, GOLF CUSTOMS, TRADITIONS, AND BUSINESS GOLF

1 RULES

- I suggest that you learn the etiquette of golf rather than trying to learn all the rules.

- As a beginner, when you play with players who are better than you, you'll gradually learn the rules of golf. Your companions will teach you. Learn as you go.

- You are not required to have memorized all the rules, but do buy and carry the current *USGA Official Rule Book*. Become reasonably familiar with it so you can refer to it quickly.

- Always ask if you're not sure of a rule.
- If you want to become familiar with the rules rapidly, play tournament golf.
- If someone points out a rule to you, graciously thank the person.
- But if you are being reminded again and again about rules by the same person, say, "I'm new to the game. I'm not keeping score, but thank you."

1 GOLF CUSTOMS

- Be polite.
- Compliment good shots, not just great shots.
- Say "Thank you" when you're complimented, even if you thought your shot was only average.
- Smile. Have fun. Enjoy yourself.
- Shake hands with all those in your group and thank them for the game immediately after the round is complete.
- The best score on each hole goes first.
- Refrain from excessive talking.
- Soft spikes or not, don't walk in the line of another player.
- Don't allow a negative attitude to show or be heard. Keep your excuses to yourself.
- Cheer for others.
- Get a scorecard as you start out onto a course. It often lists local rules and gives you a little map. At some courses the holes aren't numbered, and you can get lost.
- Be sure to pay your debts before leaving, usually at the nineteenth hole over a drink. Say, "I owe you two bucks," or the like.
- Keep moving and keep up.

- Always fix your ball marks (sometimes called pitch marks). In fact, I fix mine and other people's. You see professional players doing this, taking care of the course. At the end of a professional tournament, you won't see any marks on the course; the players have repaired them all. To repair your divot, replace the clump of sod as described in chapter 2. Or if there's a can of sand on your cart, use this to reseed the grass where the divot occurred.

- The person farthest from the hole goes first. *Do not* get into the habit of "ready golf," where the player who's ready first, hits first. Get ready and be ready to play your next shot.

1 TRADITIONS

- Play with white balls.
- Wear brown-and-white shoes.
- Always use a caddie if they're available, or walk and carry your own clubs.
- Buy something (socks, a towel) from the pro shop at the club where you're a guest. Do this especially at private clubs where you know it's the professional who owns the shop.
- Yell, "Fore!"
- Thank the professional after each round and find a positive comment to share about the course. He or she takes pride in the presentation of the entire facility.

1 BUSINESS GOLF

- Always give yourself the opportunity to play business golf; something may happen.
- Try for a good first tee shot, even if you have to use your 3- or 4-wood. It's impressive.

- In business golf you have the chance to build business relationships by spending four hours getting to know someone. You can observe a lot about a person on the course—how he or she responds to personal embarrassment and success with peers, for instance. You can decide whether or not you could do business with this person.

- The person who extended the invitation picks up the tab for the round, caddie, and drinks. You should plan to reciprocate your host's gesture.

- You should know how to play eighteen holes in four hours and how to move along.

- You must know how to bet and play the games the group is playing.

- Trust the honor system but take note of someone who cheats. Consider how you would or would not do business with this person.

- As a guest and the host, always carry money for tips. Tip anyone who picks up your bag a dollar or two. Tip the locker room attendant. Let that person shine your shoes, and tip for this service. Always tip the outside service people such as the cart boys. These kids live off your tips. Be generous.

- Arrive forty-five minutes before your tee time so you can change shoes, warm up, and be ready.

- Call ahead to ask about shorts length, shirt collar rules, and whether you must have soft spikes on your shoes. If so, arrive with extra time in order to replace your spikes.

- Always offer to pay for yourself. Be like one of the guys.

- If you are the host, pay for everything, including tips.

- Learn to tease and learn not to take teasing personally.

- Send a thank-you note with your business card. Mention any business deals that were discussed on the course. Don't let this opportunity pass you by.

- If you win against your boss, don't make a big deal out of it. Let him or her brag or you may pay the price.
- Give putts of 2 feet or less. If you give putts too often, it may appear that you expect your companions to give putts to you. I recommend not giving 5-foot putts. Be gracious about it.

Epilogue

Golf is still a traditional game with traditional points of view, some of which are discriminatory. I'm not talking about the traditions of etiquette or being supportive of the caddie program. I mean the traditions that have made it difficult for women and minorities to have access to private courses. This is changing, although slowly. But I feel hopeful, especially when I see the gains made by players who represent minority groups, like Si Re Pak, the South Korean rookie who won the 1998 U.S. Women's Open, going into the record books as the youngest champion ever at age twenty.

Tiger Woods's Masters win really pushed golf across racial and ethnic barriers. It's great to see him out there, inspiring so many young people of all races. It's also exciting that in 1998 an Asian-American man, Vijay Singh, won the PGA trophy for the first time.

Nancy Lopez, the charismatic player of the 1970s and 1980s, has been an incredible gift to the game of women's golf. She was a great champion, entering the Hall of Fame by the time she was thirty-four years old. Now having young Si Re as a role model will, I think, inspire many other young women to explore the game and become devoted to it.

I encourage you to support the LPGA and PGA professionals at the local courses where you play. These people have worked hard for their professional status and must spend effort and dollars to keep their skills current and maintain their status with professional accreditation. Engage their services as instructors and be sure to thank them for their help.

I also want to encourage you to explore upscale daily-fee courses, and ask about nine-hole rates. You'll be paying a premium price, but it may be well worth it.

Now for my acknowledgments, which are heartfelt. I feel that Sam and I truly started this book in 1994, but God really helped us finish it. We struggled to complete it near the end. But *we* made it. We're grateful.

I want to thank Jack Baker, head professional of the Presidio Golf Club in San Francisco, and Dave Anderson, head professional at the Golf Club at Quail Lodge in Carmel, for believing that women are an important part of their staff, and for promoting women and women's golf at their facilities. I am so pleased to be a part of the staff each of these men leads.

The Presidio Golf Club has a marvelous staff of professionals plus a marvelous teaching staff. It comes from the top, from Jack, who is a wonderful person as well as an outstanding professional.

I want to thank Dave Collins, one of the top one hundred teachers in the country. He was a pupil of Jim McLean. I am grateful for his encouragement and his belief in me as a teacher and as a person. He freely gives his knowledge to those who want to become quality instructors.

I want to acknowledge the person who mentored me, Fred Wetmore, a professional years ago at the Olympic Club in San Francisco. He always told me that I should work for progress, not perfection; that I should get a little better each day. He taught me that, in order to become good at something in life, I had to be persistent. In his lessons he asked me to work on things that I found difficult but that in the end, paid off. He demonstrated to me how to be a professional player and that to become a successful one, I had to play in many, many tournaments. Fred helped me feel confident enough to become a competitor at a very young age. He taught me to welcome competition. He taught me to love golf.

I want to thank my father and mother for never pushing me into golf but simply buying me clubs and telling me I could use them whenever I was ready. I loved playing golf with my father as a kid, and I enjoy being with him on the course today. I want to thank my mother for traveling to all my junior golf tournaments and putting up with my frustration after a bad round of golf.

My very first golf experience occurred when I was just eight. My mother thought it would be good for me to see Patty Berg hit a golf ball and to meet her. Mom took me out of school to attend this clinic. Patty played a nine-hole exhibition at the club. I remember her picking me out of the audience. She teed up a shot and asked me to hit it. That was my first golf shot! She definitely inspired me.

Special thanks to Ron Rhodes and Ed Haber for their support and for providing me with the opportunities I needed to become a professional. And to Lee Martin, who was the Head Golf Professional and Director of Instruction at the Quail Lodge and Golf Club. Lee taught me from the time I was fourteen until I was twenty-one, the years when I made my most notable improvements as an amateur player. We called him "The General" because he ran one heck of a "tight ship." Being a teenager and trying to stay focused on golf was not an easy task. Lee helped with the needed discipline.

I want to thank the UCLA Women's Golf Program, and the boosters and sponsors who continue to support women's athletics. Because of that program, I was able to develop my skills and prepare myself to become a professional athlete.

I want to thank my sponsor, Wilson Sporting Goods, a company that hung in there and supported me through all the years of my career. I also want to thank Footjoy for providing me with shoes. I went through a few pairs!

As a teacher I want to thank Jim Flick, who really encouraged me. I asked Jim, "How can I become a good teacher?" He replied, "You must do two things. First, go wherever you can to give at least a thousand lessons a year, and second, spend time with the best teachers and learn from them." This was advice I heard and put into practice.

I really want to thank Larry Dornish, the head professional at Muirfield Village in Columbus, Ohio. Larry is one of the great head professionals in the country. He always has an excellent staff of professionals. I enjoyed being part of that team.

Merle Breer was instrumental in my rookie year on tour. She took me under her wing and taught me how to hit a pitch shot and a lob shot, and how to play a practice round. She taught me a lot about the etiquette of the tour and about competition. I was a rookie and alone out there; Merle made sure I was okay.

I remember her asking me what the worst part of my game was. I told her it was my putting. She then asked me how I thought I could improve it, and I told her by spending an hour each day practicing putting. She said, "Probably." For the next few years, I must've spent two hundred hours each year putting. I worked on straight 6-foot putts and become one of the best putters on the women's tour.

I want to acknowledge Mike Adams of the PGA National Golf Academy for his method of teaching chipping.

Finally, I want to thank our publisher, Peter Burford, for seeing our vision and for supporting the concept of Three-Shot Golf.

References

Frazier, Mark. *Five Fundamentals of Golf Psychology.* Unpublished manuscript, 1996.

Murphy, Michael. *Golf in the Kingdom.* Viking Penguin, 1972.

Rotella, Bob, with Bob Cullen. *Golf Is a Game of Confidence.* Simon & Schuster, 1996.

Seligman, Martin. *Learned Optimism.* Pocket Books, 1990.

———. *The Optimistic Child.* Harper Perennial, 1995.

Shoemaker, Fred. *Extraordinary Golf.* G. P. Putnam & Sons, 1996.

Glossary

Address—The position and posture of the body relative to the ball and club just before the club moves.

Anatomical snuffbox—The little indentation between the two ligaments at the base of your thumb that is visible when you arch your thumb back toward your wrist.

Angles of approach—The degree of angle at which the club is approaching the ball, either upward or downward, or steep or shallow.

Arm swing—One of the three power generators.

Arc—Starting from the ball, the path the clubhead travels as it swings away from the ball, back toward the ball, and through the ball to the finish.

Backswing (also called **take-away**)—The portion of a swing that begins when the clubhead moves away from the ball and extends to the point at which the arm swing and the golf club reach the top of the swing.

Ball striking—The act of hitting the golf ball.

Bogey—To play a hole with a score of 1 stroke over par.

Caddie—A person who carries the clubs for you.

Centeredness of hit—How accurately the clubhead hits the ball squarely at impact.

Chip—A short-game shot near the green that has more roll than air time.

Clubface—The area of the club that makes contact with the ball.

Clubhead—The entire portion of the end of a club, including the clubface.

Clubhead speed—The speed at which the clubhead is traveling at impact.

Clubshaft—The portion of the club from its grip end to its head.

Divot—The chunk of grass that flies through the air when you take a swing that not only hits the ball, but the ground as well. A correct divot is when the chunk of grass occurs *after* the ball is struck not before.

Downswing—The portion of the swing from the top of the swing to impact.

Fairway woods—A collection of clubs, named *woods* for the material from which they were originally made, consisting of a 3-wood through a 9-wood.

Fairway wood shot—A full-swing shot made from the tees or grass using a fairway wood.

Fat shot—Ouch! This golf shot hits the ground before it hits the ball. It doesn't feel very good. Technically, the golf club hits the bottom of the arc before it gets to the ball.

Finish position—The final position of your body at the end of a swing.

Forward swing—The portion of the swing from impact to the finish position.

Full swing—The largest swinging motion that you make.

Graphite—A strong but lightweight material that is used in manufacturing clubheads and clubshafts.

Grip pressure—The amount of "squeeze" your fingers put on the handle of the golf club at the start of the swing and throughout.

Greens—Areas of short grass around each hole.

Hosel—The place on a club where the clubhead is attached to the clubshaft.

Inclined plane—The correct orientation that the golf club must follow in a full swing: swinging on a 45-degree angle to the ground and around in an arc.

Irons—A collection of clubs consisting of the 3-iron through the sand wedge.

Lag a putt—Make a long putt with the objective of leaving the ball near the cup.

Leverage—The power or force created by the wrist hinge and club shaft, with clubhead speed being the end result.

Lie—The location of the ball on the ground; the different ground conditions on which the ball is sitting.

Lob wedge—A lofted club used for sand play and extremely high-trajectory shots.

Loft—The upward angle of a clubhead.

Lofted club—A club that angles upward.

Lower-body motion—The pivot or turning of the hips, legs, and feet during a swing.

LPGA—Ladies' Professional Golf Association.

Mid-iron—The middle-length irons (7-iron, 6-iron, 5-iron).

Miniature swing—A swing that has a shorter backswing and downswing than a full swing; a swing motion that moves in the lower one-third of the arc.

Open stance—When the left foot is dropped back from the toe line at the setup position, this can also open the hips and shoulders slightly, causing them to aim left of the target line as well.

Outcome goal—A goal that focuses on outcomes or results, such as the score for a round; you have less control over an outcome goal than a performance goal.

Performance goal—A goal that focuses on what you have control over, like your attitude about learning or how often you practice.

PGA—Professional Golfers' Association.

Pitch shot—A short-game shot that has more air time than ground time, used to get the ball over an obstacle.

Pitching wedge—A lofted club used in pitching.

Pivot—The torso and hip rotation.

Posture—The way the body is held at address.

Power generators—Three factors that influence the outcome of a golf shot.

Pre-hinge engagement—The small amount of left-hand wrist hinge at the setup position.

Preshot routine—A set of steps carried out before swinging the club; ideally, these steps will become habits that don't have to be consciously thought out.

Putt—A short-game shot played on the green with the objective of getting the ball into the hole in 1.

Putter—The funniest looking golf club in your bag. It is usually the shortest, heaviest, and the club with the least clubface loft. It is designed to roll the ball along the ground or "green" which is also referred as the "putting surface."

Sand wedge—A lofted club used in sand play.

Setup—How you are positioned before swinging the club, including grip, posture, placement of the feet, and placement of the ball.

Shank—A shot in which the ball is hit by the club's hosel, causing the ball to fly immediately right of the target line.

Shape of the shot—The curve, distance, and direction of a shot.

Short-iron—The shorter-length irons (sand wedge, pitching wedge, 9-iron, 8-iron).

Shotmaking—Executing shots well.

Slice—A shot that curves dramatically from left of the target line to right of the target line

Spine elevation—The angle of your spine at address—that is, how bent over you are from the hips.

Stance—The position of the feet in the setup.

Sweet spot—The very best place on the clubface with which to strike the ball.

Target line—An imaginary line between the ball and the target.

Tee shot—The first shot on every hole, played between two markers from the teeing ground. You have a choice, on this shot only, to take the advantage of placing the ball on a small peg called a "tee."

Titanium—A strong but lightweight material that is used in manufacturing clubheads and clubshafts.

Title IX—Federal legislation that secured more access for women to advantages previously enjoyed only by men—for example, athletic scholarships.

Top shot—A shot in which the ball is struck at its midpoint or higher.

Trajectory—The flight of the ball; the launch angle of the ball.

Up and down—In chipping, attempting to get onto the green and down into the hole in 2.

Upswing—The motion of the club from the lowest point of the arc to the follow-through.

Waggle—The feel of the clubhead in your hands during the preshot routine.

Width of stance—The distance the feet are apart at the address position (this changes depending on the size of the swing).

Wrist hinge—The 90-degree angle made by the clubshaft and the left forearm as you grip the club and begin to swing; one of the three power generators.

Index

Made in the USA